Module 8

Assessment for Prevention and Early Intervention (K–3)

LETRS

Language Essentials for Teachers of Reading and Spelling

Louisa C. Moats, Ed.D.

SOPRIS WEST EDUCATIONAL SERVICES
A CAMBIUM LEARNING COMPANY

BOSTON, MA • LONGMONT, CO

ISBN 1-59318-196-5

Printed in the United States of America

Published and Distributed by

SOPRIS
WEST™
EDUCATIONAL SERVICES

A Cambium Learning™ Company

4093 Specialty Place • Longmont, CO 80504 • (303) 651-2829
www.sopriswest.com

191MOD8/11-05

Dedication

To my husband, Steve Mitchell, whose support is constant and invaluable.

Acknowledgments

The LETRS modules have been developed with the help of many people. Our active national trainers, including Carol Tolman, Susan Hall, Marsha Davidson, Anne Cunningham, Marcia Berger, Deb Glaser, Linda Farrell, Judi Dodson, and Anne Whitney have all offered valuable suggestions for improving the module content and structure. Their devotion to delivering LETRS across the country is appreciated beyond measure. Bruce Rosow, Kevin Feldman, Susan Lowell, Patricia Mathes, Marianne Steverson, Lynn Kuhn, Jan Hasbrouck, and Nancy Eberhardt contributed their expertise to the first edition and continue to provide essential input and feedback. Many other professionals from all over the country who have attended institutes and offered constructive criticism have enabled our response to educators. I hope you see your ideas reflected in the revised editions of this continually evolving material.

I am grateful for the daily support and energy of the Sopris West office staff, editors, and designers including Lynne Stair, Sue Campbell, Sandra Knauke, Christine Kosmicki, and Kim Harris. Special thanks are due to Toni Backstrom, who manages the LETRS program with enthusiasm, competence, and commitment.

Stu Horsfall, Ray Beck, Steve Mitchell, Chet Foraker, and Steve Kukic are the vision and energy behind the publication of evidence-based programs in education that will help all children learn. I am so fortunate to be working with all of you.

—LCM

About the Author

Louisa C. Moats, Ed.D., is a nationally recognized authority on how children learn to read and why people fail to learn to read. Widely acclaimed as a researcher, speaker, consultant, and trainer, Dr. Moats has developed the landmark professional development program LETRS for teachers and reading specialists. She recently completed four years as site director of the NICHD Early Interventions Project in Washington, D.C., which included daily work with inner city teachers and children. This longitudinal, large-scale project was conducted through the University of Texas, Houston; it investigated the causes and remedies for reading failure in high-poverty urban schools. Dr. Moats spent the previous fifteen years in private practice as a licensed psychologist in Vermont, specializing in evaluation and consultation with individuals of all ages who experienced difficulty with reading, spelling, writing, and oral language.

Dr. Moats began her professional career as a neuropsychology technician and teacher of students with learning disabilities. She later earned her master's degree at Peabody College of Vanderbilt University and her doctorate in reading and human development from the Harvard Graduate School of Education. She has been licensed to teach in three states. Louisa has been an adjunct professor of psychiatry at Dartmouth Medical School and clinical associate professor of pediatrics at the University of Texas at Houston.

In addition to LETRS (Sopris West, 2004), her authored and co-authored books include:

- *Speech to Print: Language Essentials for Teachers* (Brookes Publishing, 2000),

- *Spelling: Development, Disability, and Instruction* (York Press, 1995),

- *Straight Talk About Reading* (Contemporary Books, 1998),

- *Parenting A Struggling Reader* (Random House, 2002),

- *Spellography* (Sopris West, 2003),

- *TRIP: The Reading Intervention Program* (Sopris West, in development).

Louisa has also published numerous journal articles, chapters, and policy papers including the American Federation of Teachers' "Teaching Reading is Rocket Science," the Learning First Alliance's "Every Child Reading: A Professional Development Guide," and the report on the D.C. Early Interventions Project: "Conditions for Sustaining Research-Based Practices in Early Reading Instruction" (with Barbara Forman), *Journal of Remedial and Special Education*, 2004. She continues to dedicate her professional work to the improvement of teacher preparation and professional development. She is the consulting director of literacy research and professional development for Sopris West Educational Services. Louisa and her husband divide their time between homes in Colorado, Idaho, and Vermont. Their extended family includes a professional skier, a school psychologist, an alpaca rancher, and an Australian Shepherd.

Contents for Module 8

Overview of LETRS: Language Essentials for Teachers of Reading and Spelling

LETRS is designed to enrich and extend, but not to replace, program-specific professional development for teachers of reading and language arts. Teachers who implement a core, comprehensive reading program must know the format and instructional routines necessary to implement daily lessons. Teaching reading is complex and demanding, and new teachers will need both modeling and classroom coaching to implement the program well. Program-specific training, however, is not enough to enable teachers to tailor instruction to the diverse needs in their classrooms. Even teachers who are getting good results will need to understand the research-based principles of reading development, reading differences, and reading instruction. Reaching *all* learners through assessment and intervention is only possible when the teacher understands who is having difficulty, why they might be struggling, and what approaches to intervention are grounded in evidence. An empowered teacher is one who knows and can implement the best practices of the field, as established by a scientific research consensus.

The American Federation of Teachers' *Teaching Reading Is Rocket Science* and the Learning First Alliance's *Every Child Reading: A Professional Development Guide* provided the blueprint for these modules. LETRS modules teach concepts about language structure, reading development, reading difficulty, and assessment practices that guide research-based instruction. The format of instruction in LETRS allows for deep learning and reflection beyond the brief "once over" treatment the topics are typically given. Our professional development approach has been successful with diverse groups of teachers: regular classroom and special education, novice and expert, rural and urban.

The modules address each component of reading instruction in depth—phonological and phonemic awareness; phonics, decoding, spelling, and word study; oral language development; vocabulary; reading fluency; comprehension; and writing—as well as the links among these components. The characteristics and the needs of second language learners (ELL), dialect speakers, and students with other learning differences are woven into the modules. Assessment modules teach a problem-solving strategy for grouping children and designing instruction.

Teachers usually need extended time to learn and apply the knowledge and skills included in LETRS, depending on their background and experience. The content is dense by design. Each module is written so that teacher participants will engage in questions, problems, and tasks that lead to understanding, but understanding may occur in small steps, gradually, over several years. Some of the modules also are accompanied by the LETRS Interactive CD-ROMS, self-instructional supplements for independent study and practice, developed with the help of a grant from the SBIR program of the National Institute for Child Health and Human Development.

More information about LETRS material, programs, and institutes is available at www.letrs.com.

Content of LETRS Modules Within the Language-Literacy Connection

Components of Comprehensive Reading Instruction	Organization of Language						
	Phonology	Morphology	Orthography	Semantics	Syntax	Discourse and Pragmatics	Etymology
Phonological Awareness	2	2					
Phonics, Spelling, and Word Study	3, 7	3, 7, 10	3, 7, 10				3, 10
Fluency	5		5	5	5		
Vocabulary	4	4	4	4	4		4
Text Comprehension		6		6	6	6, 11	
Written Expression			9, 11	9, 11	9, 11	9, 11	
Assessment	8, 12	8, 12	8, 12	8, 12	8, 12	8, 12	

Objectives

◆ Familiarize teachers with four uses for assessments.

◆ Explore in depth the use of screening and progress-monitoring as a basis for instructional decision-making.

◆ Become familiar with the content and procedures of a screening test for young children.

◆ View and practice interpreting screening data for the purpose of making instructional decisions.

◆ Examine spelling errors, writing samples, and other informal assessments in the context of case study analysis.

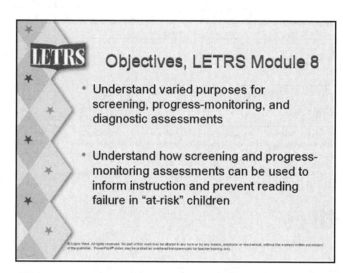

Slide 1

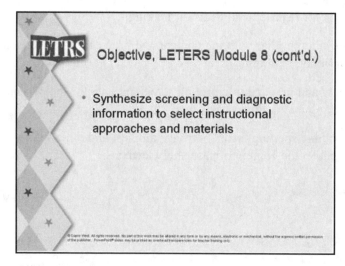

Slide 2

Slide 3

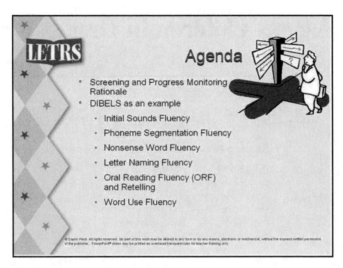

Slide 4

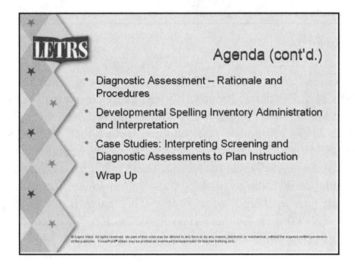

Slide 5

Why Assess Children in Grades K-2?

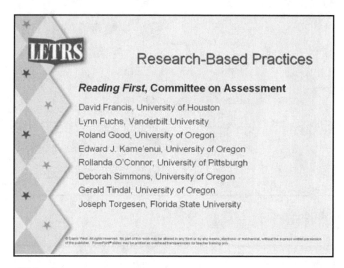

Slide 6

National concern over reading failure has been rising since the National Assessment of Educational Progress (NAEP) has consistently shown high rates of reading failure among fourth and eighth graders. In high poverty areas, up to 70% of minority, poor children cannot read at even a "basic" level. In middle class communities, about 38% to 40% of students are failing to score at even a "basic" level in reading. They do not have even partial mastery of foundational reading skills and thus are not able to function at "grade level" or fully participate in their schooling. This reality is one of the primary causes of membership in the underclass in our society—the group for whom there are few opportunities for educational or economic advancement. The good news, however, is that reading is teachable if instruction is comprehensive, sufficiently intensive, and includes practices supported by research.

New tools are now available to locate "at risk" children before they fail, and to focus educators on the children's instructional needs. Recently validated early screening instruments, including the Dynamic Indicators of Basic Early Literacy Skills (DIBELS, the University of Oregon and Sopris West), the Texas Primary Reading Inventory (TPRI, The Texas Education Agency), Fox in a Box (McGraw-Hill), and the PALS test of the University of Virginia and Virginia Department of Education are grounded in two kinds of research: (a) research on the prediction of reading difficulty in young children; and (b) research on what is taking place in the minds of people who are learning to read.

Scientists in many disciplines—cognitive psychology, neuropsychology, school psychology, language development, medicine, and education—have achieved consensus on how children acquire reading skill, why some children have difficulty learning to read, and what kind of instruction is likely to help most children learn (National Reading Panel, 2000). Good screening assess-

ments measure the foundation skills whose ability to predict later reading fluency and comprehension is established (Rayner et al., 2001).

The realization that reading skill is necessary for school success and that most reading problems can be prevented and ameliorated if they are caught early has driven many state and federal reading initiatives. Important research reviews (Armbuster, Lehr, & Osborn, 2001; National Reading Panel, 2000; Rayner et al., 2001; Snow, Burns, & Griffin, 1998), policy statements (American Federation of Teachers, 1999; Learning First Alliance, 2000), and legislation (Reading Excellence Act, 1999; Reading First, No Child Left Behind, 2001) promote early identification and intervention with students in the "basic" and "below basic" categories of reading achievement. DIBELS, TPRI, Fox in a Box, and others are valuable tools for allocating instructional resources to those who need them most.

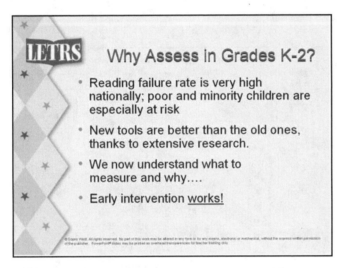

Slide 7

The road to reading success begins early in life. Early experiences with language stimulation, books, and the world outside home predict to a great extent how likely it is that a child will be a good reader. In addition, knowledge of letters, awareness of speech sounds in words (phoneme awareness), and the ability to link the two (the alphabetic principle) are prerequisites for early reading. These can be measured before the child actually learns to read. Even students with good preschool preparation are not immune to reading failure because reading demands linguistic and symbolic skills in which they may be weak. Moreover, those students with poor preparation for school in language, print awareness, or worldly experience will demonstrate signs of risk as soon as they enter school. Preschool programs such as Head Start are not enough to inoculate children against reading failure (Zigler & Styfco, 1994).

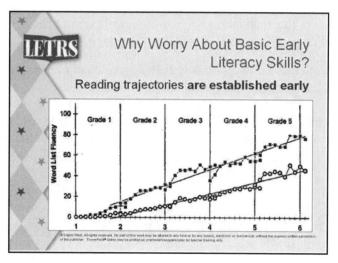

Slide 8

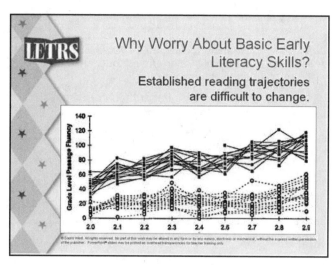

Slide 9

Thus, we need to do more than prepare children for school entry. We need to know how far they have progressed on the pathway to strong reading development so that we can intervene right away if they are falling behind the research-based benchmarks for growth. If we help students early, they are less likely to experience social, behavioral, or motivational problems that often accompany reading difficulty (Good, Simmons, & Kame'enui, 2001). Children who are below benchmark skill levels in reading by the end of first grade have a 1 in 4 to 1 in 7 chance of ever catching up to grade level without intensive and costly intervention.

> *We can catch children before they fail and intervene successfully; children should not have to fail before they come to our attention and receive preventive instruction.*

Types of Assessments

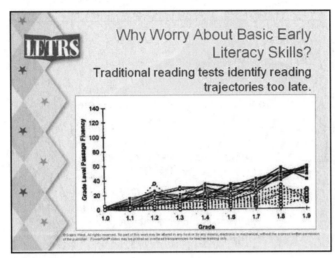

Slide 10

Children who are falling behind in reading can be located during the first month of first grade, or even before that. Tests we commonly use, however, are insensitive to month-by-month growth or small differences in relative standing that will become big differences as months go by. Changing our approach so that we find children early will require the use of new tools.

Slide 11

Four types of assessments are reviewed in this module—each used for specific purposes.

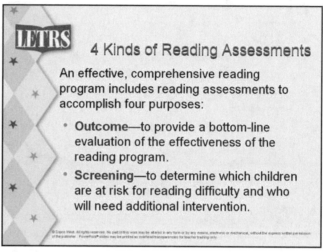

Slide 12

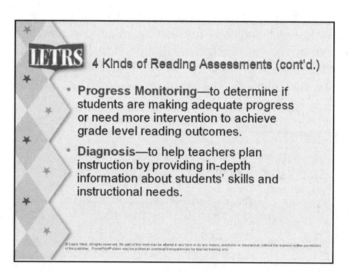

Slide 13

Outcome or summative assessments are "high stakes," end-of-year account-ability tests, now required of states who are complying with the provisions of the No Child Left Behind legislation. They usually measure reading achieve-ment with silent passage reading and multiple choice comprehension questions. They are given to groups and are usually given under time constraints. Scores are reported as standard scores, percentiles, and normal curve equivalents, so that consumers can tell where an individual stands in relation to normative data for that age group. New state initiatives and those funded with Reading Excellence, Title 1, School Improvement, and Reading First funds require districts to demonstrate improvement with students "at risk." End-of-year tests, such as the Stanford 9, Iowa Test of Basic Skills,

Terra Nova, and Metropolitan Achievement Tests are often used for this purpose. Accountability systems often rely on such tests to show overall progress within a state, district, or school.

Outcome tests given by districts and states reflect the end result of curriculum design, program implementation, and individual teachers' efforts over the course of an entire school year. The problem, of course, is that by the end of third or fourth grade when the summative tests are usually given, it is too late to plan and implement a more effective instructional program without considerable cost and effort. Intervention with older students takes much more time and is much more expensive and difficult to implement than early intervention with kindergarten and first grade students (Torgesen et al., 2001). Schools can and should know how many students are likely to meet state standards far in advance of the spring date on which the high stakes tests are given.

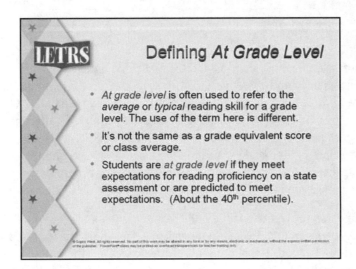

Slide 14

A new definition of "grade level" will be necessary to interpret the results of screening measures. Grade level is a minimal proficiency target that predicts a passing score on the high stakes outcome test. Over and over, studies continue to find that target to be about the 40th percentile. A screening test can tell us how likely it is that a student will be at grade level at the end of each year.

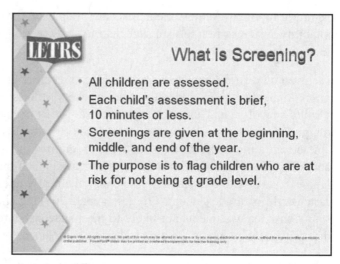

Slide 15

Screening assessments, such as DIBELS, are designed to identify at-risk children efficiently and effectively *before they fail or before they establish a pattern of failure*. Such measures should be used to intervene and help the at-risk children achieve at grade level. Early identification of children at risk is possible because the scores on measures such as DIBELS are good predictors of performance on high-stakes, summative tests. DIBELS and measures like it enable teachers to intervene with students at risk for failure *before* they take end-of-year assessments.

In the standards movement of the late 1990's, many states rewrote their literacy standards to enumerate component skills that must be mastered by students learning to read. Respecting current research on the nature of reading acquisition, many states included standards on both underlying or component reading skills, such as letter recognition, phonological awareness, and reading fluency, and higher level comprehension skills, such as the ability to summarize a passage or evaluate an author's tone. Both component skills and the deployment of those skills for higher purposes are important to measure in a screening assessment and both are highly interrelated.

The "simple" skills measured by DIBELS and TPRI, such as timed letter naming and timed nonsense word reading, predict eventual reading comprehension so well that testing only needs to take 7 to 15 minutes per child and costs much less than more elaborate testing approaches.

◆ "Simple" tasks predict complex reading skills very well, especially if the measures reflect accuracy and speed.

◆ What is tested is simpler than what is taught: Both foundational skills and comprehension will need to be taught, even though comprehension may not be tested thoroughly.

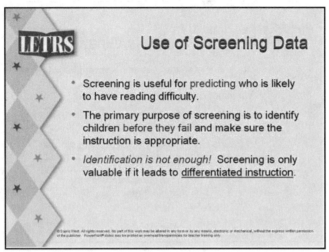

Slide 16

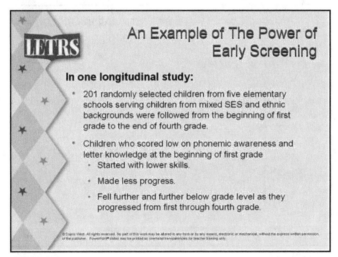

Slide 17

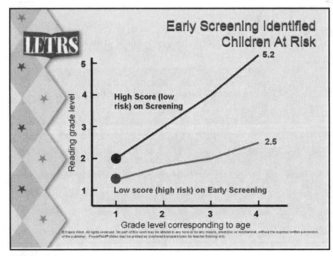

Slide 18

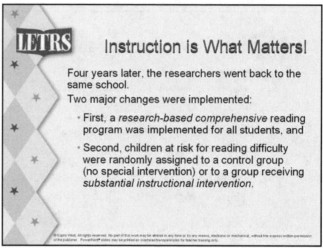

Slide 19

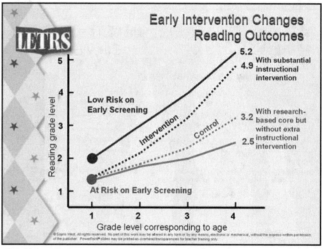

Slide 20

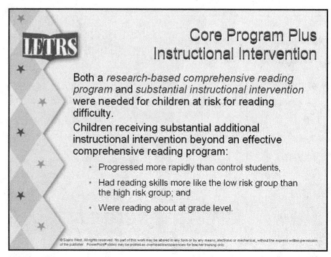

Slide 21

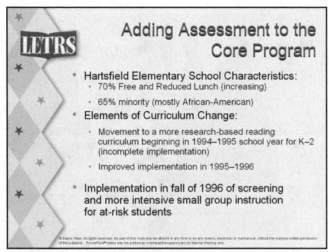

Slide 22

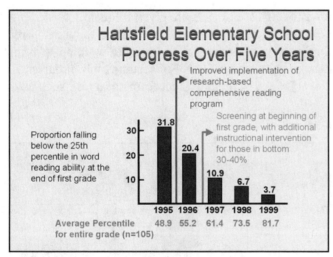

Slide 23

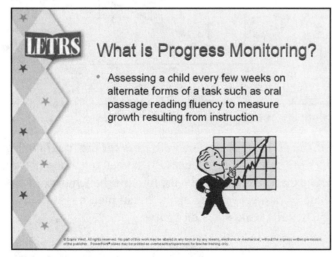

Slide 24

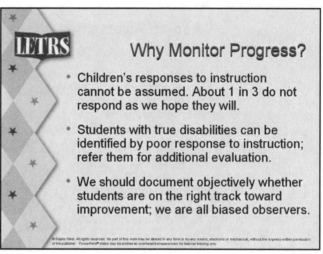

Slide 25

Progress-monitoring assessments are given frequently to students who have been screened and found to be at risk for reading failure. In order to determine whether a given instructional program is working to bring the child closer to a target or benchmark level of reading skill, progress is monitored as much as every week with equivalent forms of a task such as oral reading fluency.

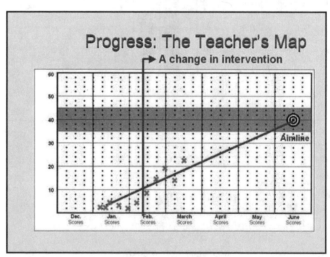

Slide 26

In this figure, the child made minimal progress for the first month of instruction (January) on oral reading fluency. If something does not change, the child will not be on course to achieve the minimal benchmark of 40 words per minute by June of first grade. The instructional plan might need to be modified to ensure that the child stays on course.

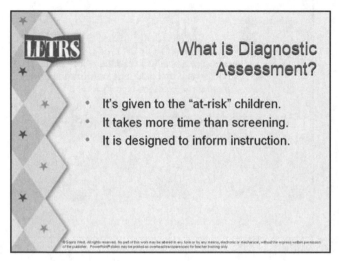

Slide 27

The term **diagnostic assessment** has two meanings: First, it refers to the use of informal surveys and standardized tests that probe a child's academic knowledge and skill in depth so that teachers can be specific in their instructional planning. Second, it refers to the activity of classifying a handicapping condition or disorder according to the diagnostic criteria established by a profession such as psychiatry or psychology.

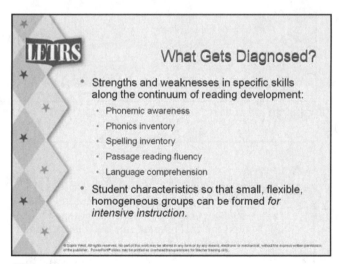

Slide 28

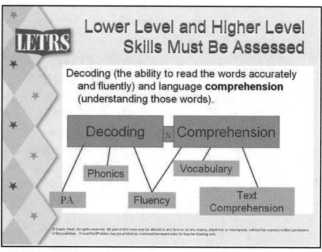

Slide 29

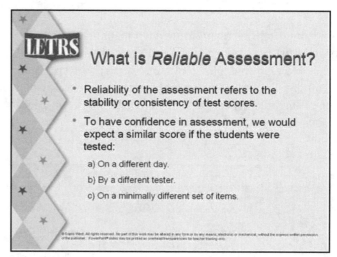

Slide 30

Slide 31

In order to be most useful in a school setting, assessments of any kind must meet certain psychometric criteria. The most important are reliability, validity, and efficiency. A reliable measure is likely to yield the same result if it were to be given several times on the same day in the same context. A valid measure corresponds well to other known, valid measures (concurrent validity) and predicts with good accuracy how students are likely to perform on an accountability measure (predictive validity). An efficient measure can be given with relatively low cost in relatively little time.

Slide 32

Dynamic Indicators of Basic Early Literacy Skills (DIBELS®)

The Dynamic Indicators of Basic Early Literacy Skills (DIBELS) are brief but powerful measures of the critical skills that underlie early reading success. Supported by two decades of sophisticated research by Roland Good, Ruth Kaminski and others at the University of Oregon, these simple assessments predict how well children are likely to be doing in reading comprehension by the end of third grade. Three or four short tasks at each grade level, K–3, help teachers locate, monitor, and intervene with at-risk students in kindergarten through third grade. DIBELS assessment is a proven approach for taking "vital signs" of reading health and pointing teachers in the direction of effective teaching.

Teachers or other personnel trained to administer the assessment give the screenings individually to all students in a grade within a short time frame. Screenings, called Benchmark Assessments, should occur three times per year.

Slide 33

Screening and Progress-Monitoring: Two Uses for DIBELS

DIBELS assessments enable early identification of children with potential problems, but more importantly, DIBELS enables educators to modify their approach if a student is not on course to achieve district or state reading goals. Therefore, DIBELS fulfills two purposes: *screening* and *progress-monitoring*.

The *screening* function of DIBELS begins in kindergarten, even before students have learned to read words. It is carried out in the fall, mid-winter, and spring of each year through third grade. The *progress-monitoring* components of DIBELS are used selectively with the at-risk children on a week-to-week basis, if necessary, to determine how well they are progressing toward a goal. Again, the purpose of DIBELS is to catch the children at risk before failure sets in and to mobilize instructional support for them.

♦ All students in a class are given the DIBELS Benchmark assessments three times per year.

♦ Only the at-risk students are given the progress-monitoring assessments.

♦ DIBELS contains "measures," "assessments," or "indicators" rather than "tests" because DIBELS is a tool for planning instruction. It is designed not so much for determining a final outcome of instruction but to help improve projected outcomes.

♦ DIBELS Benchmarks are used for screening and grouping children.

♦ DIBELS Progress-Monitoring is for tracking at-risk children's response to instruction.

♦ DIBELS may need to be supplemented with other diagnostic tests if students have suspected learning disabilities.

♦ DIBELS is not a summative or comprehensive evaluation of reading achievement.

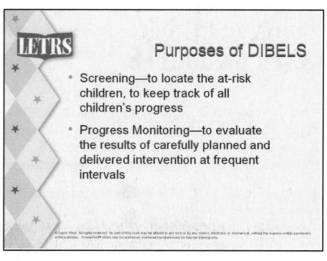

Slide 34

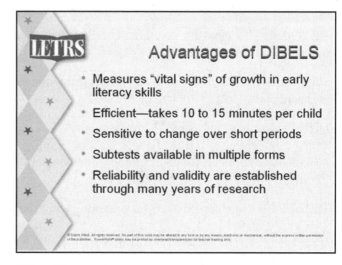

Slide 35

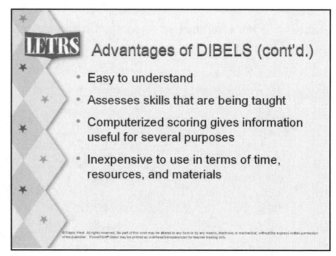

Slide 36

Advantages of DIBELS

DIBELS was developed to meet these criteria:

1. **Scores are reliable.** DIBELS developers have been careful to define the conditions of standardized administration and document the reliability of the individual measures. Thus, children's scores are likely to be truly representative of their abilities. Retesting is easy if the scores seem unrepresentative of what a child can do.

2. **Administration is economical and efficient.** The benchmarks and progress-monitoring tests are relatively simple to learn, administer, and score, and the materials are less costly than similar instruments.

3. **Computer-based scoring system can track data on individuals and groups.** The University of Oregon maintains a website (http://dibels.uoregon.edu) on which data can be entered, records kept, and results analyzed. This costs $1.00 per child at present (2004).

4. **Repeated assessment is possible.** The Benchmark tests given three times per year use different items in each subtest so there is no practice effect from taking the test several times. The progress-monitoring tools have up to 20 different "probes" or tasks that are equivalent in difficulty. A child does not repeat the same task, although testing may be frequent with alternate forms.

5. **Subtest content measures foundational reading skills established by research.** Letter knowledge, letter-sound association, phoneme awareness, syllable decoding (non-word decoding efficiency), passage reading fluency, and passage retelling are all measured directly.

6. **DIBELS scores predict success or failure on a high-stakes criterion.** Low scores on DIBELS indicate the likelihood of failure on end-of-year achievement tests; high scores indicate the likelihood of success.

7. **Subtest scores are sensitive to small gains.** The effects of good instruction (designed according to research-based principles and components) are measurable even after short intervals.

8. **Instructional goals are given for each grade and skill.** Because of extensive validation research, levels of performance on foundation reading skills can be recommended and serve as "targets" at each grade level.

9. **Decision-making about individuals is supported.** DIBELS identifies who needs help, what goals should be attained as a consequence of the instruction given, and whether the instruction is being effective week to week.

10. **Decision-making about school systems is supported.** Data from groups of at-risk individuals can be used to determine whether the instructional support system and curriculum are leading to improvement, year to year.

   ◆ Reliability and validity are established.

   ◆ Tests are efficient and economical.

   ◆ Scoring interpretation and recordkeeping done by computer.

   ◆ Repeated assessments do not spoil the results.

   ◆ Subtest content is research-supported.

   ◆ End-of-year achievement is predicted by DIBELS score.

   ◆ Instructional goals for each grade are established.

   ◆ Decision-making for individual children is facilitated.

   ◆ Decision-making around programs and curriculum is possible.

Finding the Research Base on DIBELS

The Early Childhood Research Institute on Measuring Growth and Development (ECRI-MGD) at the University of Oregon has constructed DIBELS, validated its ability to predict outcomes, and tested its reliability using data from thousands of young children in many regions of the country. The most current technical report summarizing the extensive research behind DIBELS is available from the University of Oregon (Good et al., in press).

Content of Measures: What and Why

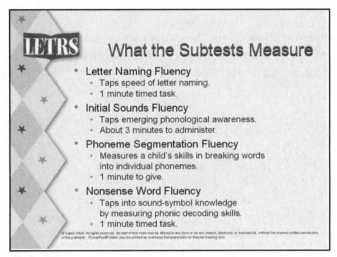

Slide 37

The foundational skills that are causally related to complex reading behavior are now well established in a large body of scientific work that has accumulated over more than thirty years from many disciplines. DIBELS is designed to sample those skills and to direct educators toward teaching those skills. Additional *diagnostic* evaluation, to be given by a teacher, learning specialist, language specialist, or psychologist, may be needed in areas where students are not making sufficient gains.

All the DIBELS are timed measures. Researchers have found repeatedly that the automaticity with which reading subskills are used and the fluency with which passages are read correlate very highly (.91) with success on traditional silent reading comprehension tests such as the Stanford Achievement Test (Fuchs & Fuchs, 2001; Wolf and Katzir-Cohen, 2001).

Slide 38

Benchmark assessments are given three times a year to all children in a grade. *Progress-monitoring* assessments are used electively when children's response to intervention needs to be closely followed.

	Word Use Fluency	Initial Sound Fluency	Letter Naming Fluency	Phoneme Segmentation Fluency	Nonsense Word Fluency	Oral Reading Fluency	Retelling Fluency
DIBELS, By Grade and Time of Year							
K, Fall							
K, Winter							
K, Spring							
K. ProgM							
1, Fall							
1, Winter							
1, Spring							
1, ProgM							
2, Fall							
2, Winter							
2, Spring							
2, ProgM							
3, Fall							
3, Winter							
3, Spring							
3, ProgM							

Progress-monitoring, 20 alternate forms at the same level of difficulty, optional for students in the at-risk category

DIBELS Indicators

1. **Letter Naming Fluency** (Kindergarten to Grade 1)

   This subtest is a powerful indicator of risk for reading failure. Students are asked to name as many letters as they can, upper and lower case randomly mixed, within one minute. The lowest 20% in a district are at high risk for failing to achieve literacy benchmarks, whereas the group between the 20th and 40th percentiles are at some risk. Long-term outcomes are greatly affected by instruction and learning opportunities.

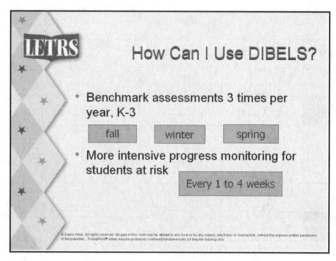

Slide 39

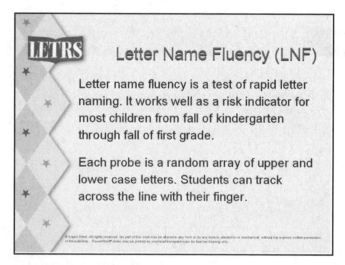

Slide 40

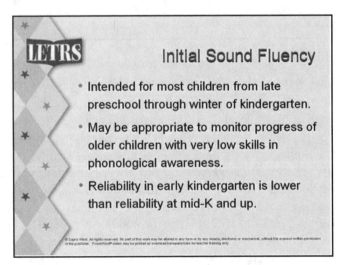

Slide 41

2. **Initial Sound Fluency** (Kindergarten)

Once called Onset Recognition Fluency, this subtest measures the child's ability to identify, isolate, and pronounce the first sound of an orally presented word. The examiner produces a sound and the child must find which of four pictures begins with that sound. For example, the examiner says, *This is a sink, cat, gloves, and hat. Which picture begins with /s/?* The child is also asked to orally produce the beginning sound for an orally presented word that matches one of the given pictures. The child's response time is measured by the examiner. The score is the number of correct initial sounds given per minute. The subtest takes about three minutes to administer. There is a separate collection of 20 alternate forms for progress-monitoring.

Initial Sound Fluency

- Intended for most children from late preschool through winter of kindergarten.

- May be appropriate to monitor progress of older children with very low skills in phonological awareness.

- Reliability in early kindergarten is lower than reliability at mid-K and up.

Slide 42

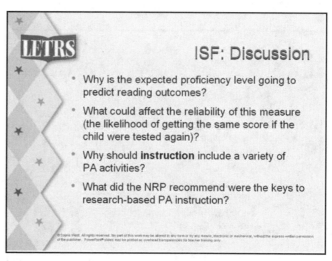

Slide 43

3. **Phoneme Segmentation Fluency** (Mid-K to End Grade 1)

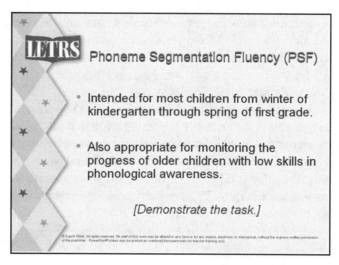

Slide 44

PSF is a direct measure of phoneme awareness. By the end of kindergarten, most children can take apart and pronounce the sounds of a three-phoneme syllable. Those who can not may be exhibiting phonological processing difficulties, a warning sign for reading difficulty. The examiner gives the child a word or syllable with three or four phonemes and asks the child to say the individual sounds that make up the word. For example, the examiner says "sat" and the child says /s/ /a/ /t/. The score is the number of correct phonemes produced in one minute. The measure takes about two minutes to administer and has 20 alternate forms for monitoring progress.

4. **Nonsense Word Fluency** (Mid-K Through Beginning Grade 2)

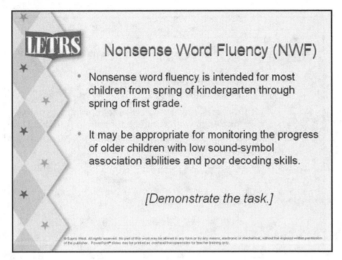

Slide 45

NWF measures the ability to link letters with sounds (the alphabetic principle) and use that knowledge to decode three-letter syllables that alone are nonsense words (sis, sil, com). The child reads randomly ordered VC (ov, ap) and CVC (sis, pom, ruv) words. The child receives credit for pronouncing individual sounds or the correct sounds in a whole syllable read as a unit. For example, the child receives three points for reading "raj" as a syllable or for saying /r/ /a/ /j/. All the vowels in the syllables are short vowels.

The score is the number of letter-sounds correct in one minute. The child who reads whole syllables will receive a higher score because the rate of correct sound production will be higher than the child who pronounces each sound separately. The child who reads whole words is more fluent; his or her phonics skills are automatized to the point of useful application in word decoding.

The subtest takes about two minutes to administer. There are more than 20 alternate forms for progress-monitoring.

5. **Oral Reading Fluency** (Mid-1st Grade to Grade 3)

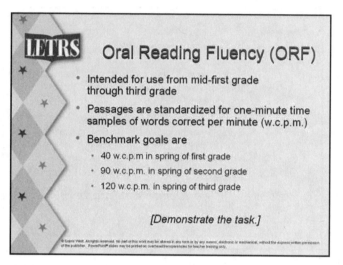

Slide 46

Benchmark passages at each grade level are used to measure accuracy and speed in oral reading of graded passages. A version of curriculum-based measurement of oral reading fluency was published as the Test of Oral Reading Fluency (Children's Educational Services, 1987). The measure is used to identify children in need of additional assessment and intervention and to monitor reading progress.

Passages are calibrated for each level. Students read each of three passages aloud for one minute. The student's score is the median correct words per minute from the three passages. Errors are words omitted or substituted, or hesitations of more than three seconds. Immediate self-corrections are scored as accurate.

Twenty alternate forms of oral reading passages are available for progress-monitoring.

6. **Oral Retelling Fluency** (Mid-1st Grade to Grade 3)

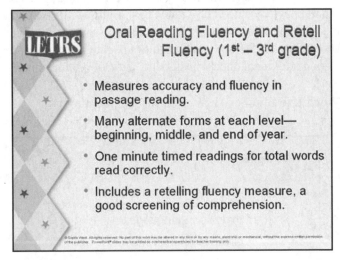

Slide 47

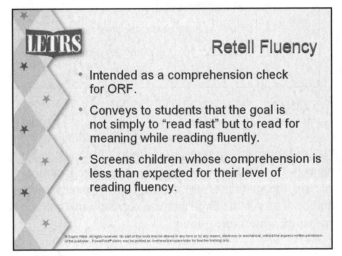

Slide 48

Designed as a check on comprehension of the passage read orally, this part of the oral reading fluency assessment asks children to tell as much as they can about what they just read. The score is the number of words the child uses to retell the story within one minute. Only words that illustrate the child's understanding of the passage are scored. (Irrelevant remarks or exclamations are not scored).

Children typically use about half the number of words in their retelling that they were able to read aloud in a one-minute timed passage. Thus, a child who reads 60 w.c.p.m. would typically use about 30 words to retell the passage. If children use less than 25% of the number of words read per minute (in this case, 15 words or fewer), there may be a specific comprehension or expressive language concern that merits further assessment.

Knowing they will need to retell the passage keeps children from thinking that oral reading fluency is simply for reading fast. The oral reading fluency score itself correlates very highly with comprehension, but the retelling adds authenticity to the assessment. Retelling correlates about .59 with the oral reading fluency score itself, indicating that it is a good additional check on students' attention to meaning.

7. **Word Use Fluency** (Fall of K Through Grade 3)

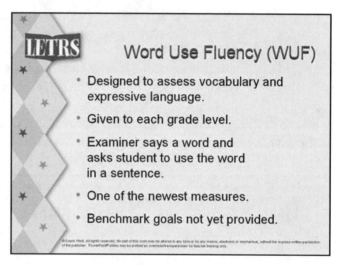

Slide 49

WUF is designed to assess vocabulary knowledge and expressive language for children at each grade level. The examiner says a word and asks the student to use the word in a sentence. The score is the number of words the child can use correctly in a phrase, sentence, or expression within one minute.

WUF is a new, experimental subtest and the designers are not quite sure what the data will show. When children are weak in this area relative to their decoding, they may have a specific problem with vocabulary and expressive language.

No benchmark goals are provided for WUF because more data need to be gathered to establish its relationship with other measures of literacy. A general rule is that students who score below the 20th percentile are at risk for poor reading outcomes, and those between the 40th and 20th percentile are at some risk.

Progress monitoring with WUF is possible at all grade levels.

Dynamic Indicators of Basic Early Literacy Skills™ 6th Ed.
Kindergarten Benchmark Assessment

Name: _____ Teacher: _____

School: _____ District: _____

	Benchmark 1 Beginning/Fall	Benchmark 2 Middle/Winter	Benchmark 3 End/Spring
Date	9-10-20___	1-30-20___	
Initial Sound Fluency			
Letter Naming Fluency			
Phoneme Segmentation Fluency			
Nonsense Word Fluency			
Word Use Fluency (Optional)	(Optional)	(Optional)	(Optional)

DIBELS® Initial Sound Fluency

This is yard, giraffe, present, bridge (point to pictures).

1.	Which picture begins with /y/?	0	1
2.	Which picture begins with /j/?	0	1
3.	Which picture begins with /pr/?	0	1
4.	What sound does "bridge" begin with?	0	1

This is crutches, feather, toothpaste, city (point to pictures).

5.	Which picture begins with /s/?	0	1
6.	Which picture begins with /f/?	0	1
7.	Which picture begins with /t/?	0	1
8.	What sound does "crutches" begin with?	0	1

This is dime, sofa, peanuts, horse (point to pictures).

9.	Which picture begins with /h/?	0	1
10.	Which picture begins with /s/?	0	1
11.	Which picture begins with /d/?	0	1
12.	What sound does "peanuts" begin with?	0	1

This is mop, footprints, dishes, goat (point to pictures).

13.	Which picture begins with /m/?	0	1
14.	Which picture begins with /f/?	0	1
15.	Which picture begins with /g/?	0	1
16.	What sound does "dishes" begin with?	0	1

Time:_____ **Seconds**   **Total Correct:** _____

$$\frac{60 \times \textbf{\textit{Total Correct}}}{\textbf{\textit{Seconds}}} = \text{_____ Correct initial sounds per minute}$$

Benchmark K.2
DIBELS® Letter Naming Fluency

S	l	u	n	s	X	k	U	x	i
l	D	H	h	T	c	r	D	g	t
u	a	n	r	U	w	C	M	J	i
n	q	R	m	t	X	O	R	B	F
s	d	l	d	w	a	f	E	F	W
X	m	z	c	j	C	Q	I	S	b
k	J	B	O	W	h	q	K	s	o
U	N	b	V	v	k	p	g	p	A
x	M	A	Z	L	u	K	G	e	V
i	Y	Y	N	P	G	T	j	Q	y
L	v	f	I	S	l	u	n	s	X

Total: _____

DIBELS® Phoneme Segmentation Fluency

Short Form Directions

Make sure you have reviewed the long form of the directions and have them available. Say these specific directions to the student:

I am going to say a word. After I say it, you tell me all the sounds in the word. So, if I say, "sam," you would say /s/ /a/ /m/. Let's try one (one-second pause)*. Tell me the sounds in "mop."*

CORRECT RESPONSE: If student says /m/ /o/ /p/, you say	INCORRECT RESPONSE: If student gives any other response, you say
Very good. The sounds in "mop" are /m/ /o/ /p/.	*The sounds in "mop" are /m/ /o/ /p/. Your turn. Tell me the sounds in "mop."*

OK. Here is your first word.

Give the student the first word and start your stopwatch.

Benchmark K.2
DIBELS® Phoneme Segmentation Fluency

hat	/h/ /a/ /t/	hear	/h/ /ea/ /r/	___/6
as	/a/ /z/	punch	/p/ /u/ /n/ /ch/	___/6
means	/m/ /ea/ /n/ /z/	by	/b/ /ie/	___/6
seam	/s/ /ea/ /m/	ship	/sh/ /i/ /p/	___/6
ought	/o/ /t/	pack	/p/ /a/ /k/	___/5
jam	/j/ /a/ /m/	if	/i/ /f/	___/5
yell	/y/ /e/ /l/	ham	/h/ /a/ /m/	___/6
calls	/k/ /o/ /l/ /z/	ear	/ea/ /r/	___/6
key	/k/ /ea/	crowd	/k/ /r/ /ow/ /d/	___/6
loud	/l/ /ow/ /d/	choose	/ch/ /oo/ /z/	___/6
bare	/b/ /ai/ /r/	bills	/b/ /i/ /l/ /z/	___/7
guy	/g/ /ie/	stand	/s/ /t/ /a/ /n/ /d/	___/7

Total: ____

Error Pattern:

DIBELS® Nonsense Word Fluency

Short Form Directions

Make sure you have reviewed the long form of the directions and have them available. Say these specific directions to the student:

Look at this word (point to the first word on the practice probe). ***It's a make-believe word. Watch me read the word: /s/ /i/ /m/, "sim"*** (point to each letter then run your finger fast beneath the whole word). ***I can say the sounds of the letters, /s/ /i/ /m/*** (point to each letter), ***or I can read the whole word, "sim"*** (run your finger fast beneath the whole word).

Your turn to read a make-believe word. Read this word the best you can (point to the word "lut"). ***Make sure you say any sounds you know.***

CORRECT RESPONSE: If the child responds "lut" or with some or all of the sounds, say	INCORRECT OR NO RESPONSE: If the child does not respond within <u>3 seconds</u> or responds incorrectly, say
That's right. The sounds are /l/ /u/ /t/ or "lut."	***Remember, you can say the sounds or you can say the whole word. Watch me: The sounds are /l/ /u/ /t/*** (point to each letter) ***or "lut"*** (run your finger fast beneath the whole word). ***Let's try again. Read this word the best you can*** (point to the word "lut").

Place the student copy of the probe in front of the child.

Here are some more make-believe words (point to the student probe). ***Start here*** (point to the first word) ***and go across the page*** (point across the page). ***When I say, "Begin," read the words the best you can. Point to each letter and tell me the sound or read the whole word. Read the words the best you can. Put your finger on the first word. Ready, begin.*** Start your stopwatch.

Benchmark K.2
DIBELS® Nonsense Word Fluency

y i z	w a n	z o c	f u l	m i k	__/15
z u m	n u f	k u n	r u v	f o d	__/15
v e p	i j	o p	j u j	s u g	__/13
z u z	o v	v i t	w a m	b u k	__/14
l e f	l u k	t e v	l o f	k o m	__/15
j u f	t a m	n o l	r e z	k e c	__/15
p u m	p o z	m u m	o l	k a v	__/14
r i v	k i c	k i s	k e m	v a k	__/15
t e k	u t	r i z	a j	v e j	__/13
y i l	j e v	n e g	s o m	j u p	__/15

Total: _____

Error Pattern:

Dynamic Indicators of Basic Early Literacy Skills™ 6th Ed.
First Grade Benchmark Assessment

Name: _____ Teacher: _____

School: _____ District: _____

	Benchmark I Beginning/Fall	Benchmark 2 Middle/Winter	Benchmark 3 End/Spring
Date			
Letter Naming Fluency			
Phoneme Segmentation Fluency			
Nonsense Word Fluency			
DIBELS™ Oral Reading Fluency[2]		(Middle score)	(Middle score)
Retell Fluency (Optional)		(Middle score)	(Middle score)
Word Use Fluency (Optional)	(Optional)	(Optional)	(Optional)

DIBELS® Oral Reading Fluency

Short Form Directions

Make sure you have reviewed the long form of the directions and have them available. Say these specific directions to the student:

Please read this (point) ***out loud. If you get stuck, I will tell you the word so you can keep reading. When I say "Stop," I may ask you to tell me about what you read, so do your best reading. Start here*** (point to the first word of the passage)***. Begin.***

Start your stopwatch when the student says the first word of the passage.

At the end of **1 minute**, place a bracket (**]**) after the last word provided by the student, stop and reset the stopwatch, and say, ***"Stop."*** (remove the passage)

If the student reads more than 10 words correct, proceed with the retell part. Say,

Please tell me all about what you just read. Try to tell me everything you can. Begin. Start your stopwatch after you say "Begin."

The first time the student does not say anything for 3 seconds, say, ***"Try to tell me everything you can."*** This prompt can be used only once.

If the student does not say anything or gets off track for 5 seconds, circle the total number of words in the student's retell and say, ***"Stop."***

At the end of **1 minute,** circle the total number of words in the student's retell and say, ***"Stop."***

Benchmark 2.1
DIBELS® Oral Reading Fluency

Spring Is Coming

It has been so cold this winter. The wind blew and blew. It	13
rained and rained. The days have been gray and dark. I had to	26
wear mittens and a hat to school every day. It even snowed	38
twice.	39
At first winter was fun. Now I'm tired of the cold. It has been	53
too cold and wet to play outside. At school, we sit in the library	67
and read during recess. After school I just stay in the house and	80
play. I don't want to play inside anymore.	88
But today was nice. The sun was shining brightly even	98
though it was still cold. The wind didn't blow. My friends and I	111
played kick ball at recess. We had to take off our jackets because	124
we were warm. We even got hot and thirsty.	133
On the way home from school I saw a purple flower on our	146
street. It was blooming in the grass. I told my mother about it.	159
She wanted me to show it to her. She bent down and touched it.	173
"Come sniff this," she said. It smelled like perfume and sun	184
all mixed together. "Spring must be right around the corner," she	195
said. "This is a crocus. It's one of the first flowers of spring."	208
I can't wait for spring.	213

Retell: _____   ORF Total:_____

⊗ • • • • • • • • * • • • • • • • • • * • • • • • • • • *	30
⊗ • • • • • • • • * • • • • • • • • • * • • • • • • • • *	60
⊗ • • • • • • • • * • • • • • • • • • * • • • • • • • • *	90
⊗ • • • • • • • • * • • • • • • • • • * • • • • • • • • *	120
⊗ • • • • • • • • * • • • • • • • • • * • • • • • • • • *	150
⊗ • • • • • • • • * • • • • • • • • • * • • • • • • • • *	180

Retell Total:_____

Dynamic Indicators of Basic Early Literacy Skills™ 6th Ed.
Second Grade Benchmark Assessment

Name: _____ Teacher: _____

School: _____ District: _____

	Benchmark 1 Beginning/Fall	Benchmark 2 Middle/Winter	Benchmark 3 End/Spring
Date			
Nonsense Word Fluency			
DIBELS™ Oral Reading Fluency	(Middle score)	(Middle score)	(Middle score)
Retell Fluency (Optional)	(Middle score)	(Middle score)	(Middle score)
Word Use Fluency (Optional)	(Optional)	(Optional)	(Optional)

From *DIBELS*®: *Dynamic Indicators of Basic Early Literacy Skills*. Reprinted by permission of the author.

Dynamic Indicators of Basic Early Literacy Skills™ 6th Ed.
Third Grade Benchmark Assessment

Name: _____ Teacher: _____

School: _____ District: _____

	Benchmark 1 Beginning/Fall	Benchmark 2 Middle/Winter	Benchmark 3 End/Spring
Date			
DIBELS™ Oral Reading Fluency	(Middle score)	(Middle score)	(Middle score)
Retell Fluency (Optional)	(Middle score)	(Middle score)	(Middle score)
Word Use Fluency (Optional)	(Optional)	(Optional)	(Optional)

DIBELS BENCHMARKS AS OF MAY 2003 NORMS

Kindergarten

	Beginning of Year		Middle of Year		End of Year	
	Performance	Status*	Performance	Status*	Performance	Status*
Initial Sound Fluency	0–3	At Risk	0–9	Deficit		
	4–7	Some Risk	10–24	Emerging		
	8+	Low Risk	25+	Established		
Letter Naming Fluency**	0–1	At Risk	0–14	At Risk	0–28	At Risk
	2–7	Some Risk	15–26	Some Risk	29–39	Some Risk
	8+	Low Risk	27+	Low Risk	40+	Low Risk
Phoneme Segmentation Fluency			0–6	At Risk	0–9	Deficit
			7–17	Some Risk	10–34	Emerging
			18+	Low Risk	35+	Established
Nonsense Word Fluency			0–4	At Risk	0–14	At Risk
			5–12	Some Risk	15–24	Some Risk
			13+	Low Risk	25+	Low Risk
Word Use Fluency (optional)	No Benchmark Goal Established Informal goal is for students in lowest 20th percentile of a district to be considered "at risk"; between 20th and 40th percentile considered "some risk"; and above 40th percentile, "low risk".					

First Grade

	Beginning of Year		Middle of Year		End of Year	
	Performance	Status*	Performance	Status*	Performance	Status*
Letter Naming Fluency**	0–28	At Risk				
	29–39	Some Risk				
	40+	Low Risk				
Phoneme Segmentation Fluency	0–9	Deficit	0–9	Deficit	0–9	Deficit
	10–34	Emerging	10–34	Emerging	10–34	Emerging
	35+	Established	35+	Established	35+	Established
Nonsense Word Fluency	0–12	At Risk	0–29	Deficit	0–29	Deficit
	13–23	Some Risk	30–49	Emerging	30–49	Emerging
	24+	Low Risk	50+	Established	50+	Established
Oral Reading Fluency			0–7	At Risk	0–19	At Risk
			8–19	Some Risk	20 - 39	Some Risk
			20+	Low Risk	40+	Low Risk
Retell Fluency (optional)	No Benchmarks Established Informal goal is 50% of words read. Students with score of 25%–50% may be considered some risk. Students with retell score of 25% or less may be considered at risk.					
Word Use Fluency (optional)	No Benchmark Goal Established Informal goal is for students in lowest 20th percentile of a district to be considered "at risk"; between 20th and 40th percentile considered "some risk"; and above 40th percentile, "low risk".					

Second and Third Grades—End of Year Goals

Oral Reading Fluency	
Performance	Status
0–49	Deficit
50–89	Emerging
90+	Established

Oral Reading Fluency	
Performance	Status
0–69	Deficit
70–109	Emerging
110+	Established

Retell Fluency and Word Use Fluency are also administered in Second and Third Grades.

* Categories "At Risk," "Some Risk," and "Low Risk" are used when progress toward an established predicting benchmark is being measured. Categories "Deficit," "Emerging," and "Established" are used when the established final predicting benchmark for that task is being measured.

** Letter Naming Fluency goals are informal and are indicators, not established predictors, of future reading abilities.

Used by permission of Susan Hall, author of *Designing Instruction With DIBELS Data, forthcoming.*

Interpreting DIBELS Data

Slide 53

Benchmark Expectations for Children's Progress

Benchmark goals and timelines for achieving them are summarized in the table below. These benchmarks have been established by research in different settings with thousands of children (Good et al., in progress; Good, Simmons & Kame'enui, 2001). The benchmarks represent *minimal* levels of satisfactory progress for the *lowest achieving* students (Good, Gruba, & Kaminski, 2001). One hundred percent of the students in the grade should achieve them if 100% of the students are to read at grade level or better. The benchmarks from grade to grade follow a progression in reading development wherein each step a child attains builds upon prior steps and is necessary for success in subsequent steps.

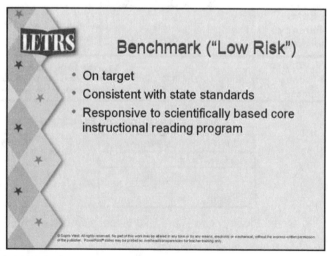

Slide 54

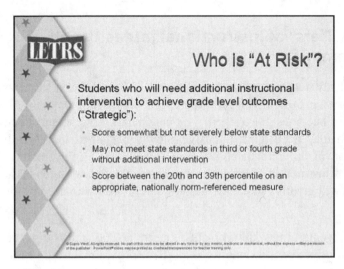

Slide 55

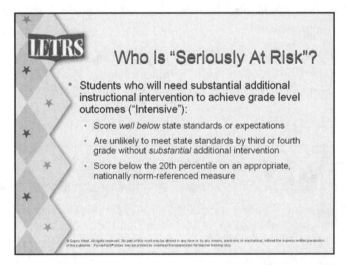

Slide 56

Making Sure Scores Are Accurate

Sometimes the benchmark test scores are inaccurate. Examiners make mistakes. Young children's test results may be unrepresentative of their actual performance because the children may be insecure, inattentive, unfamiliar with the requirements of the task, or just having a bad day. The advantage of DIBELS is that children can be easily rechecked if their group placement appears to be misjudged or the scores do not agree with one another.

The progress-monitoring booklets provide alternate testing forms that can be used to retest a child. By retesting a child on a different day or with a different examiner, we can be more confident that the scores are reliable. Two or three retests are usually enough to get a consistent picture of the child's actual level of skill.

Three "Tiers" of Instructional Intensity and Programming

The intensity and type of instruction provided to children should match the degree of their difficulty. Again, the goal is to provide that help *before* reading failure becomes entrenched. The benchmark assessment identifies children who may need more intensive, slowly paced, or individually tailored instruction in order to meet the next benchmark. Highly effective regular classroom instruction that uses a research-validated comprehensive reading program will greatly reduce the number of children who need more intensive support.

Those with emerging skills who are between the 20th and 40th percentiles can be taught effectively in small groups with programs strong on systematic, explicit instruction of foundational reading skills (letter recognition, phoneme awareness, letter-sound correspondence, phonic decoding, reading fluency). Such programs should also have strong components on vocabulary and language comprehension.

Children who score in the "deficit" or deficient range usually need one-one, one-two expert instruction with a multisensory, systematic, structured language approach that attempts to rebuild a strong foundation for learning to read.

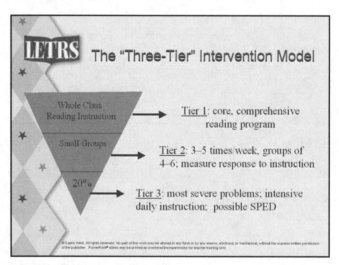

Slide 57

Examples of Approaches Designed for

Regular Classroom, Comprehensive Core Reading Programs	Second Tier Intervention, 20th–40th Percentile	Third Tier Intervention, Below 20th Percentile
Open Court (2002), McGraw-Hill	*Read Well*, Sopris West	*Road to the Code* (Brookes, Pub.)
Harcourt Brace (2002)	*Optimize* (Simmons & Kame'enui), Scott Foresman	*Wilson Fundations* (Wilson Language)
Houghton Mifflin (2002)	*Project Read* (Language Circle, Bloomington, MN)	Lindamood-Bell
Reading Mastery (SRA)	*Reading Mastery* (SRA)	Alphabetic Phonics
Read Well (Sopris West)	Phono-Graphix	Orton-Gillingham
Scott Foresman (under revision)	Spaulding Approach	Slingerland
	The Reading Intervention Program (Sopris West)	*Ladders to Literacy* (Brookes)
	WatchWord (Sopris West)	*Sound Partners* (Sopris West)
	Stepping Stones to Literacy–K (Sopris West)	

Differentiated Instruction

Teachers have many programs to choose from, and will have additional well-designed programs as research on reading instruction continues and publishers improve their products to reflect the findings of research. Other variables that matter are the size of the group, the instructional time, the amount of appropriate practice, and emphasis on the skills most important for reading progress.

Specifying Instructional Goals

The plan for an individual student should specify goals that are steps to becoming a good reader. The goals should focus on essential skills (phonological skills, letter knowledge, sound-symbol association, word decoding, passage reading fluency, retelling fluency). The plan should include the amount and type of instruction the student needs, the logistics of program implementation, and how progress will be evaluated. Need is determined by the child's place on the continuum of reading development. For example, Brandon's plan on page 53 includes a goal for improvement in phoneme segmentation fluency and an "aim line" toward the goal.

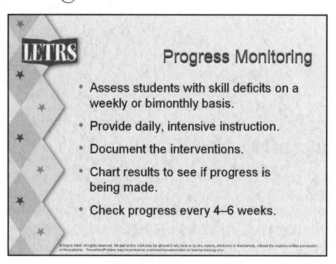

Slide 58

Evaluating and Using Progress-Monitoring Results

Slide 59

Interventions should be implemented with a progress-monitoring plan. If instruction is not having the desired effect, something should be changed to enable the child to progress more steadily toward the goal, if possible. In evaluating the effectiveness of an intervention, the following steps are recommended.

1. Decide how often progress-monitoring assessments will be given. The children with the greatest deficits should be assessed weekly. Others can be assessed every 4–6 weeks.

2. Establish a rule for deciding whether progress is satisfactory. For example, if three weekly assessments in a row indicate that the student is below the "aim line" of progress toward the goal, a change in approach is indicated. The instruction may need to target different skills, be more intensive, or use another type of instructional routine.

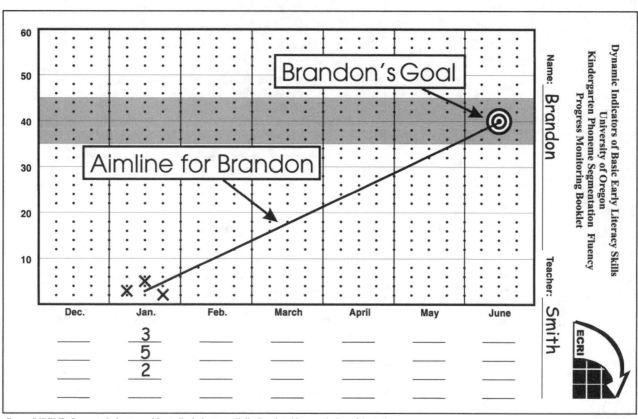

From *DIBELS®: Dynamic Indicators of Basic Early Literacy Skills*. Reprinted by permission of the author.

How Do I Get Started?

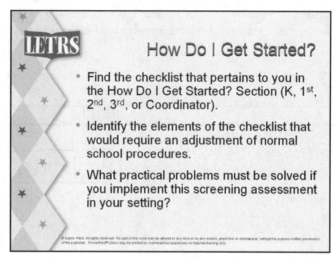

Slide 60

If I am a kindergarten teacher . . .

◆ Read Administration and Scoring Guide.

◆ Have a stopwatch and clipboard.

◆ Attend workshop on administration; role-play and give practice tests with a team to ensure that scores will be accurate.

◆ Obtain Benchmark Scoring Booklet for each child in the class.

◆ Obtain two copies of student response material (one in reserve).

◆ Make an envelope or folder for each child in the class; children will be retested with the same Benchmark Scoring Booklet up to three times.

◆ Determine whether fall, winter, or spring assessments will be given. This depends on the *time of year*, not whether you are doing the assessments for the first, second, or third time.

◆ Arrange schedule to allow time to assess each child.
  - Fall Benchmarks (ISF, LNF)   4 minutes/child
  - Winter Benchmarks (ISF, LNF, PSF)   7 minutes/child
  - Spring Benchmarks (ISF, LNF, PSF & NWF)   9 minutes/child

◆ Arrange booklets in alphabetical order to facilitate data entry.

◆ Check booklets against class roster.

◆ Test any students remaining.

- Enter data into the computer (U. of Oregon website: http://dibels.uoregon.edu).

- Obtain reports; file and/or distribute reports to appropriate personnel.

- Discuss results with grade level team, coach, and/or administrator.

- Make instructional decisions.

- Use progress-monitoring assessments to graph at-risk children's progress toward an established goal.

If I am a 1st Grade teacher ...

- Read Administration and Scoring Guide.

- Have a stopwatch and clipboard.

- Attend workshop on administration; role-play and give practice tests with a team to ensure that scores will be accurate.

- Obtain Benchmark Scoring Booklet for each child in the class.

- Obtain two copies of student response material (one in reserve).

- Make an envelope or folder for each child in the class; children will be retested with the same Benchmark Scoring Booklet up to three times.

- Determine whether fall, winter, or spring assessments will be given. This depends on the *time of year*, not whether you are doing the assessments for the first, second, or third time.

- Arrange schedule to allow time to assess each child.
  - Fall Benchmarks (LNF, PSF, NWF)   7 minutes/child
  - Winter Benchmarks (PSF, NWF, ORF)   9 minutes/child
  - Spring Benchmarks (NWF, ORF)   7 minutes/child

- Arrange booklets in alphabetical order to facilitate data entry.

- Check booklets against class roster.

- Test any students remaining.

- Enter data into the computer (U. of Oregon website: http://dibels.uoregon.edu).

- Obtain reports; file and/or distribute reports to appropriate personnel.

- Discuss results with grade level team, coach, and/or administrator.

- Make instructional decisions.

◆ Use progress-monitoring assessments (ORF passages) to graph at-risk children's progress toward an established goal.

If I am a 2nd Grade or 3rd Grade teacher . . .

◆ Read Administration and Scoring Guide.

◆ Have a stopwatch and clipboard.

◆ Attend workshop on administration; role-play and give practice tests with a team to ensure that scores will be accurate.

◆ Obtain Benchmark Scoring Booklet for each child in the class.

◆ Obtain two copies of student response material (one in reserve).

◆ Make an envelope or folder for each child in the class; children will be retested with the same Benchmark Scoring Booklet up to three times.

◆ Determine whether fall, winter, or spring assessments will be given. This depends on the *time of year*, not whether you are doing the assessments for the first, second, or third time.

◆ Arrange schedule to allow time to assess each child.
  – Fall Benchmarks (ORF)   5 minutes/child
  – Winter Benchmarks (ORF)   5 minutes/child
  – Spring Benchmarks (ORF)   5 minutes/child

◆ Arrange booklets in alphabetical order to facilitate data entry.

◆ Check booklets against class roster.

◆ Test any students remaining.

◆ Enter data into the computer (U. of Oregon website: http://dibels.uoregon.edu).

◆ Obtain reports; file and/or distribute reports to appropriate personnel.

◆ Discuss results with grade level team, coach, and/or administrator.

◆ Make instructional decisions.

◆ Use progress-monitoring assessments (ORF passages) to graph at-risk children's progress toward an established goal.

If I am coordinating schoolwide data collection . . .

◆ Schedule data collection about two weeks after major vacations or breaks. Plan around other major events on the school calendar.

◆ Decide on an approach to data collection.

– In each teacher's class, teacher and assistant set aside 30 minutes per day for four days to test each child.

– Schoolwide, a large team of trained people set up in a central location (library, cafeteria) and test all children in a day.

– A core team of 4–8 trained evaluators goes to each classroom and assists the teacher in collecting the data in one day.

– Grade-level teams coordinate their schedules so that one teacher calls out and assesses her students while the class is visiting neighboring classes for instruction.

◆ Provide training for all data collectors.

◆ Ensure that data collectors have stopwatches, clipboards, and testing materials.

◆ Ensure that data collectors have role-played and practiced testing with team observers.

◆ Post data collection schedule at least a week ahead of time.

◆ Ensure that each student on each class roster has a booklet and data will be filed alphabetically in appropriate storage container.

◆ Contract with University of Oregon for data analysis and reporting. http://dibels.uoregon.edu

◆ Determine who will enter the data after testing is completed.

◆ Have extra materials available on day of testing.

◆ Remind data collectors to score tests as they give them; do not leave scoring for later.

◆ Organize booklets alphabetically by classroom; check against class roster.

◆ Enter data into the computer. http://dibels.uoregon.edu

◆ File student testing booklets for future use.

◆ Obtain reports and set up meeting to discuss and present results.

◆ Distribute reports appropriately and file a master copy that will not be lost.

◆ Use data for instructional decision-making.

◆ Determine who will be monitored with progress-monitoring tests; determine instructional goals and a schedule for checking children's progress.

Schoolwide Decision-Making With DIBELS

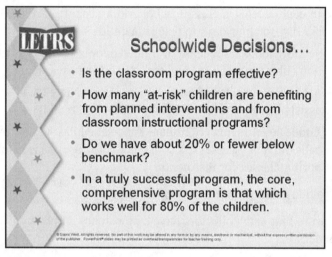

Slide 61

When regular classroom instruction is effective, about 20% of the children are still likely to need either small group or intensive instruction. If more than 20% of the children are failing to achieve benchmarks, then the program or its implementation probably need to be changed. The DIBELS website issues a report back to schools that answers the question, *What percent of students achieved essential reading outcomes?*

Following is an example of districtwide first grade reading outcomes for two successive academic years showing the distribution of scores on words read correct per minute on oral reading fluency (ORF).

In addition, a "benchmark linkage" report shows how groups of children are progressing on the critical indicators of future reading success. Benchmark linkage shows the relationship between the students' achievement of earlier benchmark goals and their achievement of later benchmark goals. The graph on page 60 shows the relationship between the achievement of initial sound fluency benchmarks (ISF) in a mid-kindergarten group and the achievement of phoneme segmentation fluency benchmarks (PSF) in spring of kindergarten for the same class.

Schoolwide Decision-Making With DIBELS®

When regular classroom instruction is effective, about 20% of the children are still likely to need either small group or intensive instruction. If more than 20% of the children are failing to achieve benchmarks, then the program or its implementation probably need to be changed. The DIBELS Web site issues a report back to schools that answers the question: *What percent of students achieved essential reading outcomes?*

Below is an example of districtwide first grade reading outcomes for two successive academic years showing the distribution of scores on words read correct per minute on oral reading fluency (ORF).

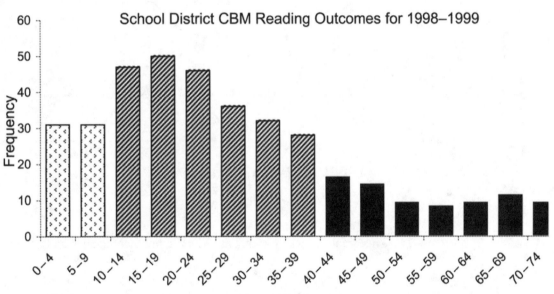

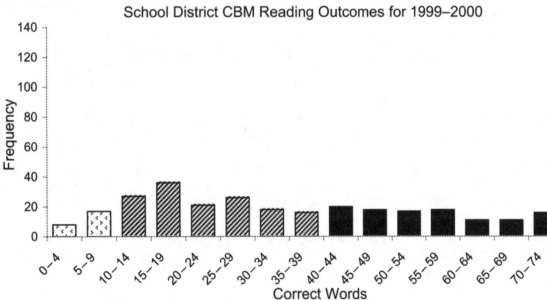

From DIBELS®: Dynamic Indicators of Basic Early Literacy Skills. Reprinted by permission of the author.

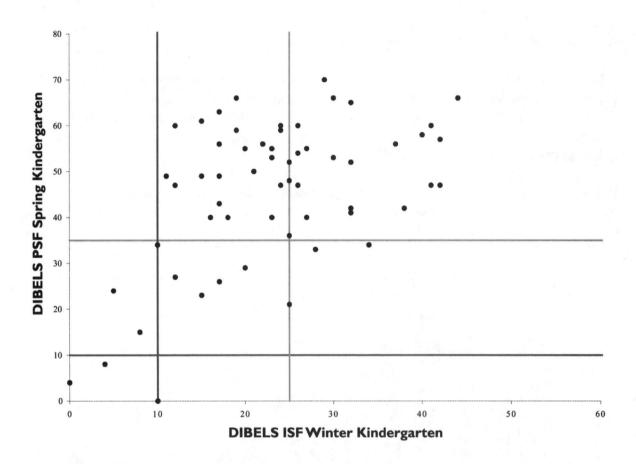

This graph shows that students who did not meet the earlier benchmark of initial sounds fluency in mid-kindergarten were also unlikely to meet the spring benchmarks on phoneme segmentation fluency. Students who were on track in identifying initial sounds in mid-kindergarten were then likely to learn to segment all of the sounds in spoken syllables. Four students in the class shown above remained severely deficient on both foundational skills and were candidates for intensive instruction beginning in first grade.

Benchmark linkage reports not only inform each teacher about the progress of each child, but also inform administrators about the effectiveness of the school's curriculum. For example, a linkage report may show that students in a school began kindergarten with strong letter naming skills, but because the instructional program did not include systematic teaching of individual speech sounds in words, students were no longer on course for achieving later reading goals by the end of kindergarten. Conversely, a linkage report can show that students began with a weakness on a benchmark, but because instruction was concentrated on accelerating progress, students actually gained ground in relation to the next benchmark.

In summary, linkage reports show if more than the expected number of students are having trouble with a specific foundation skill, then the curriculum or its implementation may need to be changed. Not all changes will lead to improvements, however; such decisions should be informed by an understanding of reading psychology, reading development, and the theoretical underpinnings that link the major components of effective reading instruction.

Technical Characteristics of DIBELS

A series of studies have investigated the reliability, predictive validity, concurrent validity, construct validity, and item sensitivity of DIBELS. Coefficients of reliability and validity can be found in Good, Gruba, and Kaminski (2001) and in Good et al. (forthcoming).

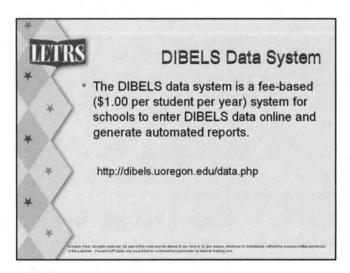

Slide 62

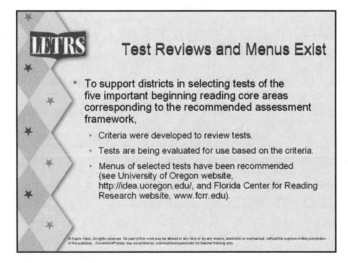

Slide 63

Interpretive Exercises–Kindergarten Class Report

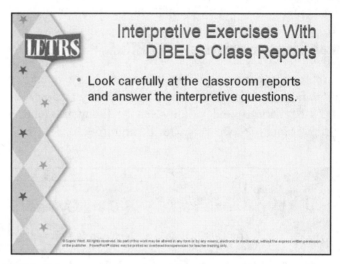

Slide 64

1. Find a student who is weak in isolating initial phonemes but who can name letters well.

2. Find three students who are stronger in phoneme isolation (ISF) than they are in letter naming.

3. How many students are below the 40th percentile in both phoneme isolation (ISF) and letter naming?

4. Which student is below average in word use fluency (WUF) but strong in phoneme isolation (ISF) and letter naming? What might that pattern of results indicate?

5. Why are the rankings based on ISF scores primarily?

6. If only 3 of 18 are at benchmark, what does that indicate?

7. How many letters must a child name to qualify as "low risk" in September?

8. How many children come into kindergarten knowing NO letter names?

Dynamic Indicators of Basic Early Literacy Skills, University of Oregon Class List Report

School: _____ District: _____ Grade: __K__ Class: _____ Assessment: _September_ Academic Year: _2002–2003_

Note: Scores provide an indication of performance only. If there is any concern about the accuracy of scores for an individual, performance should be verified by retesting with problem validation materials.

Name	Initial Sound Fluency			Letter Naming Fluency			Word Use Fluency			Instructional Recommendation
	Score	%	Status	Score	%	Status	Score	%	Status	
Student 1	0	8	At Risk	0	20	At Risk	0	32		Intensive—Needs Substantial Intervention
Student 2	0	8	At Risk	0	20	At Risk	0	32		Intensive—Needs Substantial Intervention
Student 3	0	8	At Risk	0	20	At Risk	0	32		Intensive—Needs Substantial Intervention
Student 4	2	20	At Risk	0	20	At Risk	0	32		Intensive—Needs Substantial Intervention
Student 5	2	20	At Risk	2	51	Some Risk	0	32		Intensive—Needs Substantial Intervention
Student 6	3	27	At Risk	15	85	Low Risk	0	32		Strategic—Additional Intervention
Student 7	4	34	Some Risk	0	20	At Risk	0	32		Intensive—Needs Substantial Intervention
Student 8	4	34	Some Risk	1	43	At Risk	0	32		Intensive—Needs Substantial Intervention
Student 9	5	41	Some Risk	3	56	Some Risk	7	78		Strategic—Additional Intervention
Student 10	5	41	Some Risk	4	60	Some Risk	0	32		Strategic—Additional Intervention
Student 11	6	47	Some Risk	1	43	At Risk	0	32		Intensive—Needs Substantial Intervention
Student 12	8	56	Low Risk	9	72	Low Risk	11	90		Benchmark—At Grade Level
Student 13	9	61	Low Risk	7	68	Some Risk	4	71		Strategic—Additional Intervention
Student 14	9	61	Low Risk	11	78	Low Risk	12	92		Benchmark—At Grade Level
Student 15	10	68	Low Risk	0	20	At Risk	8	82		Strategic—Additional Intervention
Student 16	11	75	Low Risk	11	78	Low Risk	0	32		Benchmark—At Grade Level
Student 17	15	85	Low Risk	0	20	At Risk	0	32		Strategic—Additional Intervention
Student 18	17	92	Low Risk	0	20	At Risk	2	66		Strategic—Additional Intervention

LNF: 90% of active students in the district have been recorded.
WUF: 90% of active students in the district have been recorded.

From *DIBELS®: Dynamic Indicators of Basic Early Literacy Skills*. Reprinted by permission of the author.

Dynamic Indicators of Basic Early Literacy Skills™ 6th Ed.
Kindergarten Benchmark Assessment

Name: ___(Intensive Student)___ Teacher: _____

School: _____ District: _____

	Benchmark 1 Beginning/Fall	Benchmark 2 Middle/Winter	Benchmark 3 End/Spring
Date	9/3/02	1/13/03	
Initial Sound Fluency	2	2	
Letter Naming Fluency	2	16	
Phoneme Segmentation Fluency		4	
Nonsense Word Fluency		0	
Word Use Fluency (Optional)	(Optional) 0	(Optional) 0	(Optional)

Dynamic Indicators of Basic Early Literacy Skills™ 6th Ed.
Kindergarten—Initial Sound Fluency

Name: **(Intensive Student)**   Teacher: _____

From *DIBELS®: Dynamic Indicators of Basic Early Literacy Skills*. Reprinted by permission of the author.

65

Jan 23, 2003

Intensive Student, K

Mi Zado can run

Dynamic Indicators of Basic Early Literacy Skills™ 6th Ed.
Kindergarten Benchmark Assessment

Name: __(Strategic Student)__ Teacher: _____

School: _____ District: _____

	Benchmark I Beginning/Fall	Benchmark 2 Middle/Winter	Benchmark 3 End/Spring
Date	9/4/02	1/13/03	
Initial Sound Fluency	9	12	
Letter Naming Fluency	7	29	
Phoneme Segmentation Fluency		33	
Nonsense Word Fluency		18	
Word Use Fluency (Optional)	(Optional) 4	(Optional) 41	(Optional)

Benchmark K.2
DIBELS® Initial Sound Fluency

This is yard, giraffe, present, bridge (point to pictures).

    1.   **Which picture begins with /y/?**   0 ①

    2.   **Which picture begins with /j/?**   0 ①

    3.   **Which picture begins with /pr/?**   0 ①

    4.   **What sound does "bridge" begin with?**   0 ①

This is crutches, feather, toothpaste, city (point to pictures).

    5.   **Which picture begins with /s/?**   0 ①

    6.   **Which picture begins with /f/?**   ⓪ 1

    7.   **Which picture begins with /t/?**   0 ①

    8.   **What sound does "crutches" begin with?**   ⓪ 1

This is dime, sofa, peanuts, horse (point to pictures).

    9.   **Which picture begins with /h/?**   ⓪ 1

    10.   **Which picture begins with /s/?**   0 ①

    11.   **Which picture begins with /d/?**   0 ①

    12.   **What sound does "peanuts" begin with?**   0 ①

This is mop, footprints, dishes, goat (point to pictures).

    13.   **Which picture begins with /m/?**   0 ①

    14.   **Which picture begins with /f/?**   ⓪ 1

    15.   **Which picture begins with /g/?**   0 ①

    16.   **What sound does "dishes" begin with?**   0 ①

Time: _____133_____ **Seconds**   **Total Correct:** ___12___

$$\frac{60 \times \textit{Total Correct}}{\textit{Seconds}} = \underline{\ \ 9\ \ } \text{ Correct initial sounds per minute}$$

Progress Monitoring Results

Dynamic Indicators of Basic Early Literacy Skills™ 6th Ed.
Kindergarten—Initial Sound Fluency

Name: _____ Teacher: _____

From *DIBELS®: Dynamic Indicators of Basic Early Literacy Skills*. Reprinted by permission of the author.

69

dn23 2003

Mt sndow cph
tump

Dynamic Indicators of Basic Early Literacy Skills™ 6th Ed.
Kindergarten Benchmark Assessment

Name: __(Benchmark Student)__ Teacher: _____

School: _____ District: _____

	Benchmark 1 Beginning/Fall	Benchmark 2 Middle/Winter	Benchmark 3 End/Spring
Date	9/5/02	1/13/03	
Initial Sound Fluency	8	17	
Letter Naming Fluency	9	48	
Phoneme Segmentation Fluency		22	
Nonsense Word Fluency		13	
Word Use Fluency (Optional)	(Optional)	(Optional) 0	(Optional)

JAN 23 2003

My SHADO CAN

Rt N.

Interpretive Exercises–First Grade Class List

1. About how many letters can a low-risk child name in a minute in September of grade 1?

2. About what percentile rank in phoneme segmentation fluency (PSF) is required to be "established"?

3. Look at student #8. What are the strengths and weaknesses? What do these indicate?

4. What is the biggest difference between student #8 and student #4? Both are "intensive" but each is unique.

5. Who is good at letter naming but weak in phoneme segmentation?

6. Who is weakest in word use?

7. Out of all these children, how many are likely to succeed on a high-stakes reading test at the end of grade 3?

Dynamic Indicators of Basic Early Literacy Skills, University of Oregon Class List Report

School: _____ District: _____ Grade: 1 Class: _____ Assessment: September Academic Year: 2002–2003

Note: Scores provide an indication of performance only. If there is any concern about the accuracy of scores for an individual, performance should be verified by retesting with problem validation materials.

Name	Letter Naming Fluency			Phoneme Segmentation Fluency			Nonsense Word Fluency			Word Use Fluency			Instructional Recommendation
	Score	%	Status	Score	%	Status	Score	%	Status	Score	%	Status	
Student 1	1	4	At Risk	15	19	Emerging	2	17	At Risk	19	56		Intensive—Needs Substantial Intervention
Student 2	31	44	Some Risk	27	25	Emerging	3	19	At Risk	38	94		Strategic—Additional Intervention
Student 3	39	64	Low Risk	13	15	Emerging	4	21	At Risk	16	44		Strategic—Additional Intervention
Student 4	21	21	At Risk	0	4	Deficit	8	31	At Risk	5	26		Intensive—Needs Substantial Intervention
Student 5	22	24	At Risk	20	24	Emerging	8	31	At Risk	15	39		Intensive—Needs Substantial Intervention
Student 6	35	54	Some Risk	36	41	Established	9	36	At Risk	27	79		Strategic—Additional Intervention
Student 7	34	52	Some Risk	40	52	Established	9	36	At Risk	16	44		Strategic—Additional Intervention
Student 8	23	26	At Risk	41	55	Established	10	40	At Risk	32	85		Intensive—Needs Substantial Intervention
Student 9	43	74	Low Risk	60	98	Established	17	51	At Risk	31	84		Benchmark—At Grade Level
Student 10	25	28	Some Risk	12	12	Emerging	18	54	Some Risk	0	11		Strategic—Additional Intervention
Student 11	38	61	Low Risk	45	65	Established	18	54	Some Risk	25	74		Intensive—Needs Substantial Intervention
Student 12	36	57	Some Risk	38	45	Established	23	70	Some Risk	17	51		Benchmark—At Grade Level
Student 13	31	44	Some Risk	30	31	Emerging	24	74	Low Risk	17	51		Strategic—Additional Intervention
Student 14	64	94	Low Risk	48	77	Established	43	92	Low Risk	26	76		Benchmark—At Grade Level
Student 15	51	86	Low Risk	58	96	Established	46	95	Low Risk	38	94		Strategic—Additional Intervention
Student 16	81	>99	Low Risk	65	>99	Established	108	98	Low Risk	26	76		Benchmark—At Grade Level
Student 17	68	95	Low Risk	57	95	Established	129	>99	Low Risk	42	>99		Strategic—Additional Intervention

LNF: 90% of active students in the district have been recorded.
PSF: 90% of active students in the district have been recorded.

NWF: 90% of active students in the district have been recorded.
WUF: 90% of active students in the district have been recorded.

Interpretive Exercises–2nd Grade
Class List

1. What is the important difference between student #1 and #4?

2. How many students scored below average (50th percentile) on non-sense word fluency (NWF)?

3. Student #10 has trouble with NWF but does well in oral passage reading fluency (ORF). Does that suggest any other problem areas?

4. In this class, how many children are likely to pass high stakes reading tests at the end of third grade? What must have happened between kindergarten and now, assuming this class was like the kindergarten class reviewed earlier?

Dynamic Indicators of Basic Early Literacy Skills, University of Oregon Class List Report

School: _____ District: _____ Grade: __2__ Class: _____ Assessment: _September_ Academic Year: _2002–2003_

Note: Scores provide an indication of performance only. If there is any concern about the accuracy of scores for an individual, performance should be verified by retesting with problem validation materials.

Name	Nonsense Word Fluency			Oral Reading Fluency			Word Use Fluency			Instructional Recommendation
	Score	%	Status	Score	%	Status	Score	%	Status	
Student 1	23	5	Deficit	9	7	At Risk	53	94		Intensive—Needs Substantial Intervention
Student 2	28	11	Deficit	9	7	At Risk	0	8		Intensive—Needs Substantial Intervention
Student 3	88	77	Established	26	29	Some Risk	37	72		Strategic—Additional Intervention
Student 4	86	74	Established	38	51	Some Risk	26	39		Strategic—Additional Intervention
Student 5	117	84	Established	52	66	Low Risk	27	42		Benchmark—At Grade Level
Student 6	134	92	Established	57	70	Low Risk	35	65		Benchmark—At Grade Level
Student 7	61	50	Established	58	72	Low Risk	52	90		Benchmark—At Grade Level
Student 8	112	81	Established	64	77	Low Risk	52	90		Benchmark—At Grade Level
Student 9	85	71	Established	65	78	Low Risk	38	75		Benchmark—At Grade Level
Student 10	46	32	Emerging	73	83	Low Risk	35	65		Benchmark—At Grade Level
Student 11	119	86	Established	73	83	Low Risk	36	69		Benchmark—At Grade Level
Student 12	132	89	Established	78	87	Low Risk	65	98		Benchmark—At Grade Level
Student 13	142	95	Established	91	92	Low Risk	45	84		Benchmark—At Grade Level
Student 14	149	96	Established	94	93	Low Risk	29	52		Benchmark—At Grade Level
Student 15	203		Established	110	96	Low Risk	69	>99		Benchmark—At Grade Level
Student 16	133	90	Established	121	98	Low Risk	54	96		Benchmark—At Grade Level
Student 17	153	98	Established	130	>99	Low Risk	39	77		Benchmark—At Grade Level

NWF: 91% of active students in the district have been recorded.
ORF: 91% of active students in the district have been recorded.
WUF: 91% of active students in the district have been recorded.

From *DIBELS®: Dynamic Indicators of Basic Early Literacy Skills.* Reprinted by permission of the author.

The Role of Additional Diagnostic Testing

Students with reading disabilities are not all alike in their profile of strengths and weaknesses. Although the majority does have difficulty with phonological skills, others have primary or related difficulties with speed of word recognition. Many students with reading disabilities have coexisting and related problems with language comprehension or use. Their difficulties may extend specifically or globally to the processing of words, sentences, discourse, and pragmatics. Many have more difficulty with written expression than they do with reading. For all these reasons, additional diagnostic testing may be indicated so that intervention plans are based on a detailed understanding of all the factors that affect student learning.

Domains Addressed in a Diagnostic Assessment of a Reading Disability or Reading Difficulty[1]

Category	Includes
Family and Individual History	• Other family members who had difficulty learning to speak, read, write, and spell • Health or medical impairments to learning • Any delays in developing spoken language in preschool • Parents' concern about speech, language, motor skills, or attention span
Cognitive Ability, or Intellectual Aptitude (IQ) (now considered optional, not necessary for a diagnosis of reading disability)	• Either a Wechsler (WISC-III, WAIS-III) or Stanford-Binet IQ test; possibly the Woodcock Johnson Test of Cognitive Abilities • Test should measure individual's aptitude for learning in verbal, logical, mathematical, visual-motor, visual-spatial, symbolic, memory, and attentional domains
Specific Language Skills	• Speech sound and syllable awareness • Word pronunciation • Word retrieval • Rapid naming of letters, numbers, colors, objects • Knowledge of word meanings • Comprehension and production of sentence structure (syntax) • Expressive verbal ability, including organization of ideas, elaboration, and clarity of expression • Comprehension of what is heard and read

(continued)

(continued) **Domains Addressed in a Diagnostic Assessment of a Reading Disability or Reading Difficulty**

Category	Includes
Single-Word Decoding and Reading Fluency	• The ability to read single words out of context under timed and untimed conditions • Apply phonic word attack to reading nonsense words, timed and untimed • Oral paragraph reading fluency and accuracy
Reading Comprehension	• Timed readings of longer passages read silently • Ability to summarize, answer multiple choice questions, or complete cloze tasks (fill-in-blanks in passage)
Spelling	• Dictated spelling test (not multiple choice) • Developmental spelling inventory • Analysis of errors for speech sound omission, letter sequence confusion, and poor memory for common words
Written Comprehension	• Composition of a story or essay for students capable of writing more than a few sentences • Analysis of word choice, conceptual organization, sentence quality, elaboration of ideas, grammar, and use of punctuation and capitalization • Informal tasks such as writing a paraphrase, combining simple sentences into compound and complex sentences, writing an outline and summary of a passage, or writing part of a structured paragraph
Handwriting	• Ability to form letters, both alone and in words • Analysis of writing to see if it sits consistently on the baseline • Consistency and slant of letters • Right- or left-handed • Appropriate pencil grip • Appropriate rotation of paper • Visibility to review work previously written (especially for left-handed)

[1] From S. Hall and L. Moats, 2002, *Parenting a Struggling Reader*, NY: Random House. Adapted with permission.

Commonly Used Diagnostic Tests

Area of Functioning	Specific Skill to Test	Commonly Used Test
Reading Words	*Letter and Word Decoding* • Real words in lists • Nonsense words in lists • Knowledge of phonic associations • Decoding new words in context *Reading Whole Words* • High-frequency sight words	• Woodcock Reading Mastery Test • Woodcock-Johnson Psychoeducational Battery—3 • Weschsler Individual Achievement Test • The Test of Word Reading Efficiency • The Decoding Skills Test • The Kaufman Test of Educational Achievement • Test of Silent Word Reading Fluency
Pre-Reading Skills	*Phoneme Awareness* • Rhyming, blending, segmenting, identifying syllables and speech sounds *Alphabet Knowledge*	• Lindamood Auditory Conceptualization Test • Rosner Test of Auditory Analysis Skills • Torgesen-Bryant Test of Phonological Awareness (TOPA) • Phonological Awareness Test (LinguiSystems) • Comprehensive Test of Phonological Processing (Pro-Ed) • Texas Primary Reading Inventory • Fox in a Box
Reading Fluency and Comprehension	*Oral Reading* *Silent Reading Comprehension*	• Gray Oral Reading Test—4 • Informal Reading Inventory • Woodcock Johnson Passage Reading • Nelson-Denny (for adolescents) • Weschsler Individual Achievement Test • Kaufman Test of Educational Achievement
Spelling	*Writing Words to Dictation* *Spelling Words in Writing*	• Test of Written Spelling—4 • Wide Range Achievement Test—3 • Qualitative Inventory of Spelling Development • Analysis of written compositions
Oral Language Skills	*Listening Comprehension* • Word knowledge • Understanding sentence structure • Passage or paragraph understanding *Expressive Language* • Speed of naming • Sentence production • Describing and summarizing	• Test of Language Development • Test of Adolescent Language • Clinical Evaluation of Language Fundamentals • Test of Word Knowledge • Rapid Automatic Naming • Weschsler Individual Achievement Test

(continued)

(continued) **Commonly Used Diagnostic Tests**

Area of Functioning	Specific Skill to Test	Commonly Used Test
Writing	*Composing a Story or Narrative* *Knowledge of Symbolic Conventions*	• Test of Written Language • Weschsler Individual Achievement Tests • Test of Written Language • Test of Written Expression • Woodcock - Johnson
Intellectual Ability	*Verbal and Nonverbal Reasoning*	• Weschsler Intelligence Scale for Children—III • Stanford-Binet—IV • Woodcock-Johnson Test of Cognitive Abilities
Visual-Motor Skills	*Form Copying* *Writing*	• Bender Gestalt Test • Visual Motor Integration Test • Rey Complex Figure Drawing • Slingerland Screening Test

Recently the technical adequacy of these and other tests for diagnostic evaluations was formally reviewed by the Reading First Committee on assessment. The summary of their test reviews can be found on the University of Oregon website: http://idea.uoregon.edu

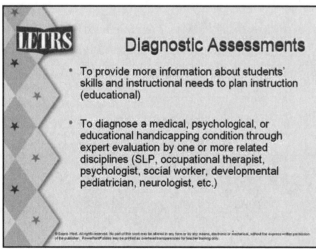

Slide 65

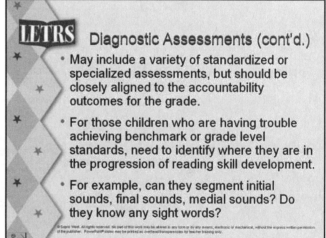

Slide 66

Slide 67

Diagnostic Surveys for Classroom Use

Finally, surveys of students' knowledge of specific language concepts and associations may be needed to know exactly where a student stands. For example, a phonics survey will inform the teacher about the sound-symbol associations the student has learned and which ones need to be taught or practiced. A spelling inventory tells which spelling conventions a student has learned along a progression of orthographic knowledge development. The Comprehensive Test of Phonological Processing (Pro-Ed) can round out the picture of phonological skill. A writing sample indicates how well a student can compose a narrative or expository text and how well the basic skills of transcription (handwriting, spelling, punctuation, organization of the work on the page) are developing. Additional language tests can help explain miscomprehensions of words, phrases, sentences, and discourse that affect listening, speaking, reading, and/or writing.

Developmental Spelling Inventory

Example: A Developmental Spelling Inventory

Learn to score the primary spelling inventory by following the instructor. Then, score any one of the three 2nd graders' tests that follow. Can you summarize the instructional needs of the student whose test you scored?

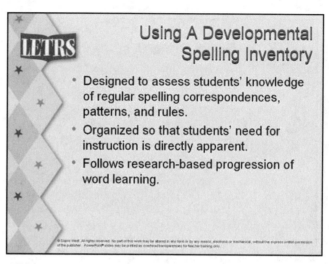

Slide 68

An efficient and valid way of determining where children might be in their acquisition of word knowledge is to use a qualitative inventory of spelling development. The first versions of these tools were validated by Edmund Henderson and his graduate students at the University of Virginia during the 1980's and 90's. Two levels of an inventory are offered here. Both were shared with this author by Dr. Francine Johnston, a coauthor of *Words Their Way* (Templeton, Bear, Invernizzi, and Johnston, 1996).

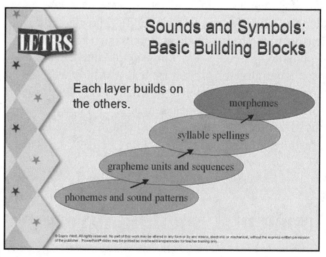

Slide 69

Directions for Administering the Spelling Inventories (from F. Johnston)

These two tests are designed to assess the word knowledge that elementary students have to bring to the tasks of reading and spelling. Students are not to study these words. That would invalidate the purpose of this inventory, which is to find out what students truly know. You can administer this same list of words three times to measure children's progress—in the fall, winter, and spring.

These words are ordered in terms of their relative difficulty for children in grades K to 5. For this reason you need only call out the words which sample features your children are likely to master during the year. However, do call out enough words to give you a sense of the range of ability in your class. For kindergarten you may only call out the first five to eight words on the primary list for most children. For the first grade call out at least 15. For second and third use the entire primary list. Use the entire elementary spelling inventory for grades 4 and 5 and for any third graders who are able to spell more than 20 of the words on the primary list. You should also call out additional words for any children who are spelling most of the words correctly at the K or first grade level.

Testing. Call the words as you would for any test. Use them in a sentence to be sure your children know the exact word. Assure your students that this is not for a grade but to help you plan better for their needs. Seat the children to minimize copying or test the children in small groups (recommended for K and early first grade).

Scoring the test. Copy a scoring sheet for each child and simply check off the features for each word which are spelled according to the descriptors at the top. Add an additional point in the "correct" column if the entire word is correct. Note that some words are scored for some features and not others and the number of possible points varies by words.

Assigning points and analyzing the results. Total the number of points under each feature and across each word. Staple the child's spelling test to the individual form. The total point score will give you a number which can be compared over time but the most useful information will be the feature analysis. Look down each feature column to determine the needs of individual students. Transfer these numbers to a class composite sheet to get a sense of your group as a whole and to form groups for instruction. Highlight children who are making two or more errors on a particular feature. For example, a child who gets 6 of 7 short vowels correct on the primary list can be considered in pretty good shape although some review work might be in order. A child who gets only 2 or 3 of the 7 short vowels needs a lot of work on that feature. Since the total possible number will vary depending on how many words you call out, the criteria for mastery will vary. I generally think like this. If X is the number of possible correct responses then X or X-1 indicates good control of the feature while X-2, or more, indicates the need for instruction. If the child did not get any points for a feature it is beyond their instructional range and earlier features need to be addressed first.

Primary Spelling Inventory—Individual Score Sheet

Name of Child: _____ Teacher: _____ Grade: _____ Date: _____ Total Points: _____

Word	Initial Consonant	Final Consonant	Digraph	Blend	Short Vowel	Long Vowel VCe	Vowel Team/ diphthong	R-control Vowel	Inflections	Correct	Word Totals
1. fan	f	n			a						
2. pet	p	t			e						
3. dig	d	g			i						
4. mob	m	b			o						
5. rope	r	p				o–e					
6. wait	w	t					ai				
7. chunk			ch	nk	u						
8. sled				sl	e						
9. stick		–ck		st	i						
10. shine			sh			i–e					
11. dream				dr			ea				
12. blade				bl		a–e					
13. coach			–ch				oa				
14. fright				fr			igh				
15. snowing				sn			ow		–ing		
16. talked							–al		–ed		
17. camping				–mp					–ing		
18. thorn			th					or			
19. shouted			sh				ou				
20. spoil				sp			oi				
21. growl				gr			ow				
22. chirp			ch					ir			
23. clapped				cl					–pped		
24. tries				tr					–es		
25. hiking									–king		

Feature Totals:

Adapted with permission from Francine Johnston and Pearson Education.

85

Assessment for Prevention and Early Intervention (K–3)

Primary Spelling Inventory—Individual Score Sheet

Name of Child: _____ Teacher: _____ Grade: _____ Date: _____ Total Points: _____

	Initial Consonant	Final Consonant	Digraph	Blend	Short Vowel	Long Vowel VC e	Vowel Team/ diphthong	R-control Vowel	Inflections	Correct	Word Totals
1. fan	f	n			a						
2. pet	p	t			e						
3. dig	d	g			i						
4. mob	m	b			o						
5. rope	r	p				o–e					
6. wait	w	t					ai				
7. chunk			ch	nk	u						
8. sled				sl	e						
9. stick		–ck		st	i						
10. shine			sh			i–e						
11. dream				dr			ea				
12. blade				bl		a–e					
13. coach			–ch				oa				
14. fright				fr			igh				
15. snowing				sn			ow		–ing		
16. talked							–al		–ed		
17. camping				–mp					–ing		
18. thorn			th					or			
19. shouted			sh				ou				
20. spoil				sp			oi				
21. growl				gr			ow				
22. chirp			ch					ir			
23. clapped				cl					–pped		
24. tries				tr					–es		
25. hiking									–king		

Feature Totals:

Adapted with permission from Francine Johnston and Pearson Education.

Primary Spelling Inventory—Individual Score Sheet

Name of Child: _____ Teacher: _____ Grade: _____ Date: _____ Total Points: _____

	Initial Consonant	Final Consonant	Digraph	Blend	Short Vowel	Long Vowel VC e	Vowel Team/ diphthong	R-control Vowel	Inflections	Correct	Word Totals
1. fan	f	n			a						
2. pet	p	t			e						
3. dig	d	g			i						
4. mob	m	b			o						
5. rope	r	p				o–e					
6. wait	w	t					ai				
7. chunk			ch	nk	u						
8. sled				sl	e						
9. stick		–ck		st	i						
10. shine			sh			i–e					
11. dream				dr			ea				
12. blade				bl		a–e					
13. coach			–ch				oa				
14. fright				fr			igh				
15. snowing				sn			ow		–ing		
16. talked							–al		–ed		
17. camping				–mp					–ing		
18. thorn			th					or			
19. shouted			sh				ou				
20. spoil				sp			oi				
21. growl				gr			ow				
22. chirp			ch					ir			
23. clapped				cl					–pped		
24. tries				tr					–es		
25. hiking									–king		

Feature Totals:

Adapted with permission from Francine Johnston and Pearson Education.

Grade: __Beginning Grade 2__   Date: __September 15__

Amanda	Camisha	9-
1. fan	1. fan	1. fan
2. pet	2. pet	2. pet
3. dig	3. dig	3. dig
4. mob	4. mob	4. mob
5. rope	5. rope	5. rope
6. wait	6. wait	6. whate
7. chunk h	7. chuck	7. chunck
8. sled	8. sled	8. slad
9. stick	9. stick	9. stick
10. shwe	10. shine	10. shine
11. drem	11. drem	11. drime
12. blade	12. blade	12. blad
13. codch	13. codch	13. coach
14. fried	14. frite	14. fright
15. snowwing	15. snowing	15. snowing
16. talked	16. talked	16. talked
17. camping	17. camping	17. caping
18. thorn	18. thorn	18. thonn
19. shouted	19. shidited	19. shateol
20. spoil	20. sporl	20. sparlyol
21. groul	21. growl	21. grnle
22. chirp	22. chirp	22. chirp
23. clapped	23. clamped	23. claped
24. tries	24. grist	24 trise
25. hiking	25. highting	25 hicing

Case Studies for Analysis and Discussion

CASE STUDY 1—LTC

Boy, age 6, evaluated in April of first grade; family history of dyslexia; fine motor awkwardness; late to learn toileting (age 4); slow to speak and had trouble articulating /r/, /l/, /th/, /s/; otherwise typical for age group. Short attention span. Scores in the middle of the average range on the Wechsler Intelligence Scale for Children (IQ 97) with strengths in abstract reasoning and weaknesses in "perceptual organization." Signs of phonological memory issues: can't remember days of the week or four seasons of the year.

SKILL ASSESSED	ASSESSMENT TOOL(S)	RESULTS
Phonological awareness	Test of Auditory Analysis Skills (Rosner)	Segments by syllable but not by phoneme.
Inventory of decoding skills		Cannot read any words.
Word reading skills	Wechsler Individual Achievement Test	21st percentile (well below average) Cannot read any whole words out of context.
Spelling assessment	Wechsler Individual Achievement Test	14th percentile (well below average) Cannot write any whole words.
	Alphabet Writing	Mixes upper and lower case letters; cannot recall g, q, v. Reverses h, j.
Oral passage reading comprehension	Gray Oral Reading	Not given
Visual-motor (form copying)	Bender Gestalt; Visual Motor Integration Test	11th percentile Copies of geometric figures are disorganized and poorly drawn.
Vocabulary development	Boston Naming Test (naming pictures of common objects)	Substitutes speech sounds while naming pictures, e.g., "pretzel" called a "princer."
	WISC-III	63rd percentile in giving word definitions.
Written expression		(see writing sample)

Spelling Responses

Child's
Name _____

Child's Responses
↓

| Dictated |

1. _____ X

2. _____ a

3. _____ dk "D"

4. _____ p

5. _____ b

6. _____ m

7. _____ no

8. _____ cat

9. _____ pig

10. _____ car

11. _____ fish

12. _____ look

13. _____ play

14. _____

15. _____

16. _____

17. _____

18. _____

19. _____

20. _____

21. _____

22. _____

23. _____

24. _____

25. _____

DISCUSSION QUESTIONS—LTC

1. What do the writing samples suggest about this child's stage of reading development? Is he pre-alphabetic, early alphabetic, later alphabetic, or beyond that? Is this child regularly representing the speech sounds in words?

2. L's teacher had been giving him word lists for spelling with "silent e" word families, such as name, game, fame. On the spelling test he wrote "nam," "fam," and "gam" when the words were dictated. How would you view those spelling attempts? What kinds of words would be appropriate for him to read and spell?

3. What type of phonological awareness instruction does this boy need (e.g., listening for syllables; onset-rime segmentation and blending; beginning phoneme identification; ending phoneme identification; complete phonemic segmentation, etc.)?

4. What other instructional components should be part of a daily, 30–45 minute intervention program?

5. We can surmise that this boy would be in the "intensive need" range of DIBELS; most children his age can read 40 words correct per minute or better. Would there have been anything to gain by screening him in kindergarten? How might his situation be different if that had happened?

CASE STUDY 2—BC

Boy, finishing third grade. On IQ testing, scored at the 95th percentile in verbal reasoning (superior), and at the 38th percentile in nonverbal, visual-spatial reasoning, such as replicating block designs. Attended very unstructured, experimental community school in first and second grades where reading was not taught systematically. Described as having no desks and allowing "personal creative freedom." Persistent problems pronouncing several speech sounds, /l/, /r/. Teacher reports that he confuses pronouns and uses the wrong past tense form of many verbs (run/ran).

SKILL ASSESSED	ASSESSMENT TOOL(S)	RESULTS
Phonological awareness	Test of Auditory Analysis Skills	Average for age
	Lindamood Auditory Conceptualization Test	Distractible, anxious, inattentive; scores at first grade level
Inventory of decoding skills	Word Attack (nonsense word reading), Woodcock Johnson Achievement Test	28th percentile (untimed) Misreads vowel sounds in *zoop, lish, feap, gusp, yosh, tayed, grawl, loast, sluke.*
Word reading skills	WJR	57th percentile (untimed)
Oral reading fluency	Curriculum-based measurement.	92 w.c.p.m. in third grade passage
Spelling assessment	WIAT Spelling	47th percentile
Silent passage reading for comprehension	California Achievement Test	38th percentile (time limited)
	Passage Comprehension, WJR	83rd percentile (untimed)
Visual-motor (form copying)	Bender Gestalt	60th percentile
Vocabulary development	Stanford Binet Vocab (oral definition of words)	84th percentile
	The Word Test	88th percentile
Written expression	WIAT Composition	6th percentile
		Gets tired and frustrated easily.
	Woodcock Johnson	Broad Written Language, 18th percentile
Expressive language	Clinical Evaluation of Language Fundamentals (Revised)	1st percentile
		Demonstrates weaknesses in formulating sentences, putting words into sentences, repeating lengthy sentences.

TEST 27

Writing Samples (cont.)

6.

it is sing

①

7.

This is a KiNe

①

8.

a bred is hachiug

⑥

9.

⓪ Chow

10. ⑴·⑸

the goo i's loking
for ne bette in the
closet

in the closet

TEST 27

Writing Samples (cont.)

11. he is opinga
    Pakeeg

12. bahqdding up a

13. and
    the boy and the
    grel are throwging
    the ball

14. they both have
    liaf

15. because

DISCUSSION QUESTIONS, BC

1. BC did poorly on nonsense word reading, guessing at most vowel sounds. How is this weakness in phonic decoding likely to affect his reading and writing?

2. BC is finishing third grade. Most of his classmates have had phonics and spelling instruction. Would you recommend that he receive phonics and spelling instruction? How would you accomplish that? Do you have a program of instruction in mind that could be implemented with a child this age?

3. Would an increase in reading fluency be a goal of instruction? How might that be accomplished?

4. Writing is a pronounced weakness for BC. How would you describe the relationship between phonemic awareness, phonic knowledge, reading fluency, comprehension, oral language expression, and writing skills in this student?

5. How do you think this child would score on DIBELS?

CASE STUDY 3—AA

Girl, age 9, third grade (May). On medication for mild ADHD. Difficulty learning her letters in kindergarten. IQ score at 73rd percentile (high average).

SKILL ASSESSED	ASSESSMENT TOOL(S)	RESULTS
Phonological awareness	Lindamood Auditory Conceptualization Test	Second grade level (mild difficulty remembering and tracking phonemes)
Inventory of decoding skills	Not given	
Word reading skills	WIAT	50th percentile Can read *jealous, ruin, comforting, afar, ideally, poise.*
Spelling assessment	WIAT	34th percentile
Silent passage reading for comprehension	WIAT (untimed)	32nd percentile
Visual-motor (form copying)	Bender Gestalt	40th percentile
Vocabulary development	WISC -III Vocab (orally given definitions)	63rd percentile
Written expression	WIAT Composition	37th percentile

AA

a b c d e f g h i j k l m n o p a r s t u v
w x y —

han	hen	pach	patch
wish		couch	couch
trap		steep	
jump		quit	cute
brav	brave	brudg	bridge
smill	~~smile~~	glar	glare
gran	grain	scrap	
crol	crawl	might	
clerk	clerk	girl	
kloch	clutch	frown	
		smock	smoke
		flock	
		stood	
		lest	least
		short	
		quiet	quite
		grap	grape
		yone	yawn
		driv	drive
		cost	coast
		hert	hurt
		pont	point
		ripe	c
		feer	fear
		pant	paint

I would like a liveing room with a kitchin Conected on to it. Two bedroomes one with a Bath room init. A grodg that would fit three cars. A addic and basment. With a offic hooked on to the grodg. A porch hoked on to the kitchin. A reke room Conected to the basment with two windos.

DISCUSSION QUESTIONS—AA

1. Do you think this student is on grade level or not? Does she need extra help? If so, how intensive should that help be?

2. According to the spelling and writing samples, does AA have unusual problems detecting the speech sounds in words?

3. To improve her spelling, decoding, and writing, AA needs continuing instruction in phoneme-grapheme correspondence, orthographic patterns, syllables, and morphemes. Which ones would you target first for direct teaching?

Table 8.1.   Student Characteristics and Instructional Needs, by Ehri's Stages of Word Knowledge Development

Pre-Alphabetic Reading and Writing	
Characteristics	**Instructional Goals and Activities**
Knows some alphabet letter names and forms. Does not understand sound-symbol correspondence (alphabetic) principle. Beginning to match words by initial consonants. May not understand concept of "speech sound." May be aware of how print looks—alternating letters, spaces, etc.	Practice alphabet matching, naming, ordering until alphabet letters can be named in random order and put in order. Practice writing the letters until alphabet can be written (a) to dictation, with model available; (b) to dictation, no model available; and (c) from memory. Use lower case for writing; upper and lower case for naming. Gain awareness of initial sounds, ending sounds, and middle sounds, leading to phoneme segmentation. Practice sound blending, first of compounds, syllables, and onset-rime units, then phonemes in one-syllable words. Associate sound with symbol, using key word or gesture if necessary. Build vocabulary through response to read-alouds and thematic content studies.
Early Alphabetic Reading and Writing	
Tries to sound out by associating sound with first letter and, perhaps, another letter or two. Wants to rely on context (pictures, topical knowledge) to guess at words. Begins to read simple sentences with known words; tries to sound out although may not get through a whole word. Attends to read-alouds, asks and answers questions and retells what reading is about. Expanding vocabulary includes the language of classroom instruction.	Blend known phoneme-grapheme correspondences into words, left to right, as groups of consonants and vowels are learned. Match all sounds on consonant and vowel charts to key words and common spellings. Acquire sight recognition of high frequency words, a few per week (goal, first 100 in first grade). Finger-point read familiar text.Retell or summarize what was read. Differentiate question words (who, what, when, where, why, how); ask and answer questions. Start to read decodable text with known letter-sound correspondences. Begin to spell high frequency words accurately and to spell regular words by sound. Learn common digraph spellings and concept of multiletter grapheme.

Later Alphabetic Reading and Writing	
Can spell words phonetically, including all the speech sounds.	Increase knowledge of rime patterns, word families, "choice" spellings for consonants, learn most common spellings for all vowel sounds.
Does not know the correct letters in many words.	Read and spell consonant blends.
Is learning the most common sight words for reading and spelling.	Read and spell words with short vowels, vowel-consonant-e, inflected endings -ed, -s, -ing.
Is starting to "chunk" common syllables and letter sequences, such as -ing, -ack.	Learn vowel teams, vowel-r patterns.
Can read decodable text, although not fluently; word-by-word reading is common.	Read decodable text with learned patterns and sight words. Increase fluency.
Can handle structured partner reading and directed reading-thinking activity.	Expand vocabulary.
	Write and publish first story books.

Orthographic Learning	
Generalizes phonics skills to unknown words, then uses context as backup.	Begin to plan before writing and stick to the plan.
Reads at least 40 words per minute in first-grade-level text.	Increase accuracy and automaticity with high frequency words and regular words for reading.
Recognizes more than 200 of the most common high frequency words.	Decode two-syllable and three-syllable words, using the most common syllable division principles.
Uses context to fully identify new words; uses context to derive meaning of new words during reading.	Increase speed to 60-90 words per minute correct in independent level reading material (95% correct).
Can employ beginning comprehension strategies—browsing, anticipating, questioning, clarifying, retelling and summarizing—with teacher support.	Expand vocabulary at rate of 800 or more words per year through second grade; increase to 2,000 words per year beginning in third grade.

Table 8.2. Scope and Sequence for Spelling (Spelling Follows Reading)

Grade Level	1	2	3	4	5	6
Beginning Consonants	b c d f g h j k l m n p qu r s t v w y z	qu ce, ci, cy ge, gi, gy				
Ending Consonants	b d g m n p t, x	-ff,-ll, -ss, -zz, -x, -ve, -ck, -ng				
Digraphs	ch, sh, th, wh	ch, tch ph, ch, gh	-ge, -dge	ph, ch in greek words		
Ending Blends	st, ft	mp, nd, nt, lf, lt, nk				
Beginning Blends	bl, cl, fl, gl, pl, sl, br, cr, dr, fr, gr, pr, tr, sc, sk, sl, sm, sn, sp, st, sw	scr, spr, squ, spl, str, tw	shr, thr	sch		
Silent Letter Spellings		kn, -lk	wr, gn	ps, rh		
Vowels	a, e, i, o, u (short vowels) a-e, i-e, o-e, u-e (long)	y as long i y as long e	schwa in 2-syllable words; eigh, ough	y as short i		
Vowel Teams	ee, ai, ay, oa, ea	ou, ow, oi, oy, au, aw, oo, eu, ew, igh	oo (foot) ui, ei, ie			
Vowel-R	er, or, ar	er, ir, ur; war, wor	err, ear, air, oar			
Inflectional Suffixes	-s, -ed, -ing (no base word change)	-s, -ed, -ing (doubling and drop -e rules)	-er, -est (comparative) change y to i rule	when rules do and do not apply	advanced doubling rule	
Prefixes			un, re	pre, en, dis, mis, ex, in	con, per, com, ad, a (chameleon prefixes)	bi, mal, circum, inter, intra, super, trans
Derivational Suffixes		-en, -hood, -ly	ment, less, ful, ness, like	tion, sion, ture, able, ous, ic, al	age, ace, ary, ence, ity, ation	-ology, -osity, -itis, -scope, plasm
Contractions	i'm, it's, don't	he'll, they've, you're, we'd				
Syllable/Morpheme Patterns	concept of syllable	compounds with 2 syllables	compounds with 2 syllables	morphemes override syllables	Latin morphemes	Greek Combining Forms

Wrap-Up

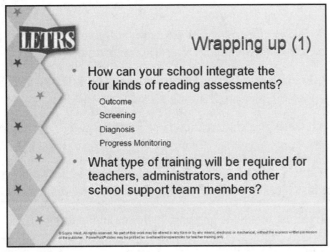

Slide 70

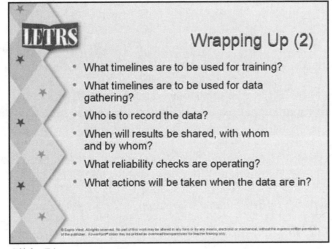

Slide 71

Bibliography

American Federation of Teachers. (1999). *Teaching reading is rocket science.* Washington, DC: Author.

Armbuster, B., Lehr, F., & Osborn, J. (2001). *Put reading first: The research building blocks for teaching children to read, kindergarten through grade 3.* Washington, DC: National Institute for Literacy.

Bear, D.R., Invernizzi, M., Templaton, S., & Johnson, F. (2001). *Words their way* (2nd Ed). Upper Saddle River, NJ: Merrill.

Foorman, B. (ed.) (2003). Presenting and remediating reading difficulties: *Bringing science to scale.* Baltimore: York Press.

Fuchs, L.S., Fuchs, D., Hosp, M., & Jenkins, J.R. (2001). Oral reading fluency as an indicator of reading competence: A theoretical, empirical, & historical analysis. *Scientific Studies of Reading, 5,* 239–256.

Good, R.H., Gruba, J., Kaminski, R.A. (2001). Best practices in using Dynamic Indicators of Basic Early Literacy Skills (DIBELS) in an outcomes-driven model. In A. Thomas & J. Grimes (Eds.), *Best practices in school psychology IV* (pp. 679–700). Washington, DC: National Association of School Psychologists.

Good, R.H., & Kaminski, R.A. (2003). *DIBELS Dynamic indicators of basic early literacy skills.* Longmont, CO: Sopris West Educational Services.

Good, R.H., Kaminski, R.A., Shinn, M., Bratten, J., Shinn, M., & Laimon, L. (n.d.). *Technical adequacy and decision-making utility of DIBELS* (Technical Report, forthcoming). University of Oregon.

Good, R.H., Simmons, D.C., & Kame'enui, E.J. (2001). The importance and decision-making utility of a continuum of fluency-based indicators of foundational reading skills for third-grade high-stakes outcomes. *Scientific Studies of Reading, 5,* 257–288.

Good, R.H., Simmons, D.C., & Smith, S. (1998). Effective academic interventions in the United States: Evaluating and enhancing the acquisition of early reading skills. *School Psychology Review, 27,* 45–56.

Hall, S. (Forthcoming). *Designing instruction with DIBELS data.* Longmont, CO: Sopris West.

Learning First Alliance. (2000). *Every child reading: A professional development guide.* Washington, DC: Author.

National Reading Panel. (2000). *Report of the National Reading Panel: Teaching children to read: An evidence-based assessment of the scientific research literature on reading and its implications for reading instruction.* Washington, DC: National Institute for Child Health and Human Development.

Rayner, K., Foorman, B.R., Perfetti, C.A., Pesetsky, D., & Seidenberg, M.S. (2001). How psychological science informs the teaching of reading. *Psychological Science, 2,* 31–74.

Reading Excellence Act. (1999). [online] Available: http://www.ed.gov/offices/OESE/REA/legis.h®l.

Shinn, M.R. (1995). Best practices in curriculum-based measurement and its use in a problem-solving model. In A. Thomas & J. Grimes (Eds.), *Best practices in school psychology III* (pp. 547–567). Washington, DC: National Association of School Psychologists.

Snow, C., Burns, S. & Griffin, P. (1998). *Preventing reading difficulty in young children*. Washington, DC: National Research Council, National Academy of Sciences Press.

Simmons, D.C., & Kame'enui, E.J. (Eds.). (1998). *What reading research tells us about children with diverse learning needs: Bases and basics*. Mahwah, NJ: Erlbaum.

Tindal, G., Marston, D., & Deno, S.L. (1983). *The reliability of direct and repeated measurement*. (Research Report 109). Minneapolis: University of Minnesota Institute for Research on Learning Disabilities.

Torgesen, J.K., Alexander, A.W., Wagner, R.K., Rashotte, C.A., Voeller, K., Conway, T., & Rose, E. (2001). Intensive remedial instruction for children with severe reading disabilities: Immediate and long-term outcomes from two instructional approaches. *Journal of Learning Disabilities*, *34*, 33–58.

Wolf, M., and Katzin-Cohen, T. (2001). Reading fluency and its intervention. *Scientific Studies of Reading*, *5*, 211–238.

Zigler, E., & Styfco, S.J. (1993). Using policy research and theory to justify and inform Head Start expansion. *Social Policy Report*, *8*(2).

Glossary

affix: a morpheme or meaningful part of a word attached before or after a root to modify its meaning; a category that subsumes prefixes, suffixes, and infixes

alphabetic principle: the principle that letters are used to represent individual phonemes in the spoken word; a critical insight for beginning reading and spelling

alphabetic writing system: a system of symbols that represent each consonant and vowel sound in a language

Anglo-Saxon: Old English, a Germanic language spoken in Britain before the invasion of the Norman French in 1066

base word: a free morpheme to which affixes can be added, usually of Anglo-Saxon origin

closed syllable: a written syllable containing a single vowel letter that ends in one or more consonants. The vowel sound is short.

concept: an idea that links other facts, words, and ideas together into a coherent whole

conjunction: a word that connects a dependent clause to a dependent clause, or a word that connects two independent clauses

consonant: a phoneme (speech sound) that is not a vowel, and that is formed with obstruction of the flow of air with the teeth, lips, or tongue; also called a closed sound in some instructional programs. English has 40 or more consonants.

consonant blend: two or three adjacent consonants before or after the vowel in a syllable, such as st-, spr-, -lk, -mp

consonant digraph: a letter combination that represents one speech sound that is not represented by either letter alone, such as sh, th, wh, ph, ch, ng

consonant-le syllable: a written syllable found at the ends of words such as *paddle*, *single*, and *rubble*

cumulative instruction: teaching that proceeds in additive steps, building on what was previously taught

decodable text: text in which a high proportion of words (around 80 to 90%) comprise sound-symbol relationships that have already been taught; used for the purpose of providing practice with specific decoding skills; a bridge between learning phonics and the application of phonics in independent reading of text

decoding: ability to translate a word from print to speech, usually by employing knowledge of sound-symbol correspondences; also the act of deciphering a new word by sounding it out

dialects: mutually intelligible versions of the same language with systematic differences in phonology, word use, and/or grammatical rules

DIBELS: *Dynamic Indicators of Basic Early Literacy Skills*, by Roland Good and Ruth Kaminski, University of Oregon

dictation: the teacher repeats words, phrases, or sentences slowly while the children practice writing them accurately

digraph: [see consonant digraph]

diphthong: a vowel produced by the tongue shifting position during articulation; a vowel that feels as if it has two parts, especially the vowels spelled <u>ou</u> and <u>oi</u>; some linguistics texts also classify all tense (long) vowels as diphthongs

direct instruction: the teacher defines and teaches a concept, guides children through its application, and arranges for extended guided practice until mastery is achieved

dyslexia: an impairment of reading accuracy and fluency attributable to an underlying phonological processing problem, usually associated with other kinds of language processing difficulties

frequency-controlled text: stories for beginning readers that use very common (high frequency) words over and over, so that the child can learn to read by memorizing a list of "sight" words; phonic patterns in the words are either secondary or irrelevant considerations

high frequency word: a word that occurs very often in written text; a word that is among the 300 to 500 most often used words in English text

generalization: a pattern in the spelling system that generalizes to a substantial family of words

grapheme: a letter or letter combination that spells a phoneme; can be one, two, three, or four letters in English (e, ei, igh, eigh)

idea generator: the thinking process that conjures up ideas as we are writing

inflection: a type of bound morpheme; a grammatical ending that does not change the part of speech of a word but that marks its tense, number, or degree in English (such as *-ed, -s, -ing*)

integrated: when lesson components are interwoven and flow smoothly together

irregular word: one that does not follow common phonic patterns; one that is not a member of a word family, such as *were, was, laugh, been*

long term memory: the memory system that stores information beyond 24 hours

meaning processor: the neural networks that attach meanings to words that have been heard or decoded

morpheme: the smallest meaningful unit of the language

morphology: the study of the meaningful units in the language and how they are combined in word formation

multisyllabic: having more than one syllable

narrative: text that tells about sequences of events, usually with the structure of a story, fiction or nonfiction; often contrasted with expository text that reports factual information and the relationships among ideas

nonsense word: a word that sounds like a real English word and can be sounded out, but that has no assigned meaning, such as *lemvidation*

onset-rime: the natural division of a syllable into two parts, the onset coming before the vowel and the rime including the vowel and what follows it: *pl-an, shr-ill*

orthographic processor: the neural networks responsible for perceiving, storing, and retrieving the letter sequences in words

orthography: a writing system for representing language

phoneme: a speech sound that combines with others in a language system to make words

phoneme awareness (also, phonemic awareness): the conscious awareness that words are made up of segments of our own speech that are represented with letters in an alphabetic orthography

phoneme-grapheme mapping: an activity for showing how letters and letter combinations correspond to the individual speech sounds in a word

phonics: the study of the relationships between letters and the sounds they represent; also used as a descriptor for code-based instruction in reading, e.g., "the phonics approach" or "phonic reading"

phonological awareness: meta-linguistic awareness of all levels of the speech sound system, including word boundaries, stress patterns, syllables, onset-rime units, and phonemes; a more encompassing term than phoneme awareness

phonological processor: a neural network in the frontal and temporal areas of the brain, usually the left cerebral hemisphere, that is specialized for speech sound perception and memory

phonological working memory: the "on-line" memory system that holds speech in mind long enough to extract meaning from it, or that holds onto words during writing; a function of the phonological processor

phonology: the rule system within a language by which phonemes can be sequenced and uttered to make words

pragmatics: the system of rules and conventions for using language and related gestures in a social context

predictable text: a story written for beginning readers that repeats phrase and sentence patterns so that the child has an easier time predicting what the words on the page will say

prefix: a morpheme that precedes a root and that contributes to or modifies the meaning of a word; a common linguistic unit in Latin-based words

reading fluency: speed of reading; the ability to read text with sufficient speed to support comprehension

risk indicator: a task that predicts outcomes on high stakes reading tests

root: a bound morpheme, usually of Latin origin, that cannot stand alone but that is used to form a family of words with related meanings

schwa: the "empty" vowel in an unaccented syllable, such as the last syllables of *circus* and *bagel*

semantics: the study of word and phrase meanings

silent letter spelling: a consonant grapheme with a silent letter and a letter that corresponds to the vocalized sound, such as *kn, wr, gn*

sound blending: saying the individual phonemes in a word, then putting the sounds together to make a whole word

sound-symbol correspondence: same as phoneme-grapheme correspondence; the rules and patterns by which letters and letter combinations represent speech sounds

speed drills: one-minute timed exercises to build fluency in learned skills

stop: a type of consonant that is spoken with one push of breath and not continued or carried out, including /p/, /b/, /t/, /d/, /k/, /g/

structural analysis: the study of affixes, base words, and roots

suffix: a derivational morpheme added to a root or base that often changes the word's part of speech and that modifies its meaning

syllabic consonants: /m/, /n/, /l/, /r/ can do the job of a vowel and make an unaccented syllable at the ends of words such as *rhythm*, *mitten*, *little*, and *letter*

syllable: the unit of pronunciation that is organized around a vowel; it may or may not have consonants before or after the vowel

text generator: the part of the mind that puts ideas into words as we are writing

transcription: the act of putting words down in writing or typing; the act of producing written words by hand once the mind has generated them

vowel: one of a set of 15 vowel phonemes in English, not including vowel-r combinations; an open phoneme that is the nucleus of every syllable; classified by tongue position and height (high-low, front-back)

whole language: a philosophy of reading instruction that de-emphasizes the importance of phonics and phonology and that emphasizes the importance of learning to recognize words as wholes through encounters in meaningful contexts

writing process approach: instruction in written expression that emphasizes a progression through three major phases, including planning and organizing the piece, writing a draft, getting feedback and revising for publication

word family: a group of words that share a rime [vowel plus the consonants that follow, such as -ame, -ick, -out]

word recognition: the ability to identify the spoken word that a printed word represents, to name the word on the printed page

Appendix

Beginning Decoding Skills Survey

BEGINNING DECODING SKILLS SURVEY
By Linda Farrell
For *The Reading Intervention Program* (TRIP)[1]

General Instructions

Record scores and errors on the Scoring Form. If the student makes an error, **be sure to record what the student reads** and how many times it takes to get the answer correct.

Directions:

1. Give the student the **Words and Sentences for Students to Read** page.

2. Ask the student to read the words at the top of the page. The student can select whether to read across or down. Stop when the student misses three in a row and ask the student if she or he can read any other words in that part of the page.

3. Ask the student to read the sentences in the middle of the page.

4. Ask the student to read the nonsense words at the bottom of the page. You may have to explain that nonsense words can be read, but they don't mean anything.

5. Record error patterns on the Error Pattern Chart.
    *   Attach the Beginning Decoding Skills Survey Scoring Form to the Error Pattern Chart.
    *   Write the specific error the student made next to the word on the Error Pattern Chart.
    *   Put a check in the box in the chart that describes student errors.

Using the Error Pattern Chart:

Teach the skills the student is missing. In general, begin by teaching the skill that is checked and furthest to the left on the grid.

---

[1] Contracted for publication by Sopris West Educational Services.

Words and Sentences for Students to Read

see	rag	rich	dust
one	lid	shop	step
play	dot	tack	trip
you	hum	whip	pond
are	bet	thin	brag

1. The cat hid in a box.
2. The fish is still in the deep lake.
3. Seven pink shellfish were in my bathtub.

vop	shap
yuz	thit
zin	chut
keb	wheck

BEGINNING DECODING SKILLS SURVEY
Scoring Form

Student name _____

Grade_____

Date of assessment _____

Assessment administrator _____

Coding
✓ = read correctly
2x or 3x = read correctly second or third time
DK = don't know
NT = not tried or skipped
Write mispronunciations, substitutions, or incorrectly read words next to or above word.

Record the number correct (include the words student read correctly the second or third time).

Real Words

Sight Words	*CVC*	*Digraphs*	*Blends*
see _____	rag _____	rich _____	dust _____
one _____	lid _____	shop _____	step _____
play _____	dot _____	tack _____	trip _____
you _____	hum _____	whip _____	pond _____
are _____	bet _____	thin _____	brag _____

Sentences

1. The cat hid in a box.

2. The fish is still in the deep lake.

3. Seven pink shellfish were in my bathtub.

Nonsense Words

CVC	*Digraphs*
vop _____	shap _____
yuz _____	thit _____
zin _____	chut _____
keb _____	wheck _____

Name _____   Grade _____   Date _____

BEGINNING DECODING SKILLS SURVEY
Error Pattern Chart

Attach the Beginning Decoding Skills Survey Scoring Form.
Cross off all words not attempted and put a check in the *No Try* box.
Write the words read incorrectly on the line next to the word attempted.
Put a check in the box in the chart that describes the error(s) for each word.

Observations: (check all that apply)
- ❑ Slow
- ❑ Guesses after trying to decode using letter-sound analysis
- ❑ Reads sound-by-sound, but cannot blend

- ❑ Quick to guess
- ❑ Possible b/d reversal

Comments (continue on back):

			Error Patterns								
Real Words		No Try	Sight Word	Consonants Initial	Consonants Final	Short Vowels	Extra Sound(s) Added	Digraphs	Blends	Long Vowels	Two Syllables
High Frequency Words											
1	see										
2	one										
3	play										
4	you										
5	are										
CVC Words											
6	rag										
7	lid										
8	dot										
9	hum										
10	bet										
Digraphs & Short Vowels											
11	rich										
12	shop										
13	tack										
14	whip										
15	thin										
Blends & Short Vowels											
16	dust										
17	step										
18	trip										
19	pond										
20	brag										
Sentences											
1	The cat hid in a box.										
2	The fish is still in the deep lake.										
3	Seven pink shellfish were in my bathtub.										
Nonsense Words											
CVC											
21	vop										
22	yuz										
23	zin										
24	keb										
Digraphs											
25	shap										
26	thit										
27	chut										
28	wheck										

BEGINNING DECODING SKILLS SURVEY
Scoring Form

Student name **Felicia**

Grade **1**

Date of assessment **April 2004**

Assessment administrator _____

Coding

✓ = read correctly

2x or 3x = read correctly second or third time

DK = don't know

NT = not tried or skipped

Write mispronunciations, substitutions or incorrectly read words next to or above word.

Real Words

Sight Words	*CVC*	*Digraphs*	*Blends*
see ✓	rag *rug*	rich *rick*	dust *duck*
one ✓	lid ✓	shop *hop*	step DK
play DK	dot DK	tack *take*	trip DK
you ✓	hum ✓	whip DK	pond DK
are *and*	bet *sounds correct didn't blend*	thin DK	brag *bag*

Sentences

1. The cat h~~i~~d *hide the* in a box.
2. The fish is ~~still in the deep lake.~~ *DK*
3. ~~Seven pink shellfish were in my bathtub.~~ *DK*

Nonsense Words

CVC	*Digraphs*
vop *vope*	shap DK
yuz DK	thit ✓
zin DK	chut
keb DK	wheck ✓

Name _Felicia_   Grade _1_   Date _April 2004_

BEGINNING DECODING SKILLS SURVEY
Error Pattern Chart

Attach the Beginning Decoding Skills Survey Scoring Form.
Cross off all words not attempted and put a check in the *No Try* box.
Write all words read incorrectly on the line next to the word attempted.
Put a check in the box in the chart that describes the error(s) for each word.

Observations: (check all that apply)

- [✓] Slow
- [ ] Guesses after trying to decode using letter-sound analysis
- [ ] Reads sound-by-sound, but cannot blend
- [ ] Quick to guess
- [ ] Possible b/d reversal

Comments (continue on back):

Real Words	No Try	Sight Word	Consonants Initial	Consonants Final	Short Vowels	Extra Sound(s) Added	Digraphs	Blends	Long Vowels	Two Syllables
High Frequency Words										
1 see										
2 one										
3 ~~play~~	✓									
4 you										
5 are *and*	.	✓								
CVC Words										
6 rag *rug*					✓					
7 lid										
8 ~~dot~~	✓									
9 hum										
10 bet *sound by sound*										
Digraphs & Short Vowels										
11 rich *rick*							✓			
12 shop *hop*							✓			
13 tack *take*					✓					
14 ~~whip~~	✓									
15 ~~thin~~	✓									
Blends & Short Vowels										
16 dust *duck*								✓		
17 ~~step~~	✓									
18 ~~trip~~	✓									
19 ~~pond~~	✓									
20 brag *bag*								✓		
Sentences										
1 The cat ~~hid~~ in ~~a~~ box. *hide the*		✓			✓					
2 The fish is ~~still in the deep lake.~~	✓									
3 ~~Seven pink shellfish were in my bathtub.~~	✓									
Nonsense Words										
CVC										
21 vop *vope*					✓					
22 ~~yur~~	✓									
23 ~~zin~~	✓									
24 ~~keb~~	✓									
Digraphs										
25 ~~shap~~	✓									
26 ~~thit~~	✓									
27 ~~chut~~	✓									
28 ~~wheck~~	✓									

BEGINNING DECODING SKILLS SURVEY
Scoring Form

Student name __Ben__

Grade __2__

Date of assessment __Feb 2004__

Assessment administrator _____

Coding

✓ = read correctly

2x or 3x = read correctly second or third time

DK = don't know

NT = not tried or skipped

Write mispronunciations, substitutions or incorrectly read words next to or above word.

Real Words

Sight Words	*CVC*	*Digraphs*	*Blends*
see ✓	rag ✓	rich ✓	dust ✓
one ✓	lid ✓	shop *hop, 2x shop*	step ✓
play ✓	dot *don't*	tack *trick*	trip ✓
you ✓	hum ✓	whip ✓	pond ✓
are ✓	bet ✓	thin ✓	brag ✓

Sentences

1. The cat hid in a box.
2. The fish is still in the ~~deep~~ *step* lake.
3. *Steven* ~~Seven~~ pink shellfish were *ed* in my bathtub. *whore*

Nonsense Words

CVC	*Digraphs*
vop ✓	shap *shep*
yuz *use*	thit *Thin*
zin *vine*	chut *crust*
keb ✓	wheck *sweek*

Name **Ben**   Grade **2**   Date **Feb 2004**

BEGINNING DECODING SKILLS SURVEY
Error Pattern Chart

Attach the Beginning Decoding Skills Survey Scoring Form.
Cross off all words not attempted and put a check in the *No Try* box.
Write all words read incorrectly on the line next to the word attempted.
Put a check in the box in the chart that describes the error(s) for each word.

Observations: (check all that apply)
☑ Slow   ☐ Quick to guess
☑ Guesses after trying to decode using letter-sound analysis
☐ Reads sound-by-sound, but cannot blend   ☐ Possible b/d reversal

Comments (continue on back):

			Consonants		Error Patterns					
Real Words		No Try	Sight Word	Initial	Final	Short Vowels	Extra Sound(s) Added	Digraphs	Blends	Long Vowels	Two Syllables
High Frequency Words											
1	see										
2	one										
3	play										
4	you										
5	are										
CVC Words											
6	rag										
7	lid										
8	dot *don't*						✓	✓				
9	hum										
10	bet										
Digraphs & Short Vowels											
11	rich										
12	shop *hop*								✓			
13	tack *trick*						✓	✓				
14	whip										
15	thin										
Blends & Short Vowels											
16	dust										
17	step										
18	trip										
19	pond										
20	brag										
Sentences											
1	The cat hid in a box.										
2	The fish is still in the deep lake. *step*				✓						✓	
3	Seven pink shellfish were in my bathtub. *Steven where*			✓				✓✓				
Nonsense Words											
CVC											
21	vop										
22	yuz *use*										
23	zin *vine*										
24	keb										
Digraphs											
25	shap *shep*						✓					
26	thit *thin*					✓						
27	chut *crust*						✓	✓	✓			
28	wheck *sweek*						✓	✓	✓			

BEGINNING DECODING SKILLS SURVEY
Scoring Form

Student name Harry

Grade 3

Date of assessment April 2004

Assessment administrator

Coding
✓ = read correctly
2x or 3x = read correctly second or third time
DK = don't know
NT = not tried or skipped
Write mispronunciations, substitutions or incorrectly read words next to or above word.

Real Words

Sight Words		*CVC*		*Digraphs*		*Blends* Very slow	
see	✓	rag	✓	rich	reach	dust	bust
one	✓	lid	lide	shop	✓	step	✓
play	✓	dot	don't	tack	take	trip	tirp
you	✓	hum	✓	whip	NT	pond	pound
are	✓	bet	bit	thin	✓	brag	brang

Sentences

1. The cat ~~hid~~ had in a box.
2. The fish is ~~still~~ silling ~~deep~~ dirt in the deep lake.
3. Seven ~~pink~~ picnic shellfish ~~were~~ where in my ~~bathtub~~ batter.   DK

Nonsense Words

CVC		*Digraphs*	
vop	voop	shap	✓
yuz	use	thit	✓
zin	✓	chut	shup
keb	keeb	wheck	wick

Name __Harry__   Grade __3__   Date __April 2003__

BEGINNING DECODING SKILLS SURVEY
Error Pattern Chart

Attach the Beginning Decoding Skills Survey Scoring Form.
Cross off all words not attempted and put a check in the *No Try* box.
Write all words read incorrectly on the line next to the word attempted.
Put a check in the box in the chart that describes the error(s) for each word.

Observations: (check all that apply)
- ☐ Slow
- ☑ Guesses after trying to decode using letter-sound analysis
- ☐ Reads sound-by-sound, but cannot blend
- ☐ Quick to guess
- ☑ Possible b/d reversal

Comments (continue on back):

			Error Patterns							
Real Words	No Try	Sight Word	Consonants Initial	Consonants Final	Short Vowels	Extra Sound(s) Added	Digraphs	Blends	Long Vowels	Two Syllables
High Frequency Words										
1 see										
2 one										
3 play										
4 you										
5 are										
CVC Words										
6 rag										
7 lid lide					✓					
8 dot don't					✓	✓				
9 hum										
10 bet bit					✓					
Digraphs & Short Vowels										
11 rich reach					✓					
12 shop										
13 tack take					✓					
14 ~~whip~~	✓									
15 thin										
Blends & Short Vowels										
16 dust bust			✓							
17 step										
18 trip tirp					✓			✓		
19 pond pound					✓					
20 brag brang					✓	✓				
Sentences										
1 The cat ~~hid~~ in a box. had					✓					
2 The fish is ~~still~~ in the ~~deep~~ lake. silling dirt								✓	✓	
3 Seven ~~pink~~ ~~shellfish~~ were in my ~~bathtub.~~ picnic N where batter		✓			✓					✓
Nonsense Words										
CVC										
21 vop voop					✓					
22 yuz use					✓					
23 zin										
24 keb keeb					✓					
Digraphs										
25 shap										
26 thit										
27 chut shup							✓			
28 wheck wick					✓					

NOTES

NOTES

NOTES

NOTES

NOTES

NOTES

NOTES